TO HONOR AND RESPECT

A PROGRAM AND RESOURCE GUIDE FOR CONGREGATIONS ON SACRED AGING

Richard F. Address

with

Andrew L. Rosenkranz

URJ Press
Department of Jewish Family Concerns
Union for Reform Judaism
New York, New York

**Union for Reform Judaism
Department of Jewish Family Concerns**

Jean Abarbanel, Chair

Mike Grunebaum, Vice-chair

Linda Wimmer, Vice-chair
and Sacred Aging Co-chair

Jacki Dwoskin, Ph.D., Sacred Aging Co-chair

The Sacred Aging project was made possible by a grant from the Charles and M. R. Shapiro Foundation of Chicago, Illinois, and by the generosity of the Toomim family of Houston, Texas, the Picheny family of Great Barrington, Massachusetts, the Wimmer family of Allentown, Pennsylvania, Gerry Bass and Susan Stahlman-Bess, and generous donations from members of Reform congregations to the Union for Reform Judaism's Fund for Reform Judaism.

Sacred Aging is a project of the Department of Jewish Family Concerns of the Union for Reform Judaism, in cooperation with Women of Reform Judaism and North American Federation of Temple Brotherhoods.

Contents

ACKNOWLEDGMENTS

To Honor and Respect is the culmination of over a year's work in congregations and regions of the Union for Reform Judaism. There are many people to thank whose work has gone into the development of the project on sacred aging. For over a year, Andrew Rosenkranz worked closely with the department's leadership, congregations, and the Sacred Aging Committee of the Department of Jewish Family Concerns. Andy's hand and devotion are evident throughout this book, and we thank him and wish him much joy and happiness in his rabbinic career.

The committee that helped develop the project was chaired with devotion and passion by Linda Wimmer and Dr. Jacki Dwoskin. Their caring helped make the development of the project a joy. They worked with a very talented group of lay leaders from the department. Harriet Rosen was part of this group, and she, as usual, shared her talents and insights as the project evolved. Likewise, we wish to thank Jay Abarbanel, Marion Adler, Les Atkinson, Jan Bergman, Davna Brook, Steve Burkett, Rabbi Paul Citrin (CCAR), Dr. Tom Cole, Dr. Joel Deutsch, Rabbi Leah Doberne-Schor, Dr. Lisa Elliot, Paula Erdelyi, Rachel Finkelman, Rachael Freed, Ina Glassberg, Ruth Goldberger, Dr. Dan Gottlieb, Jay Greenfield, John Hirsch, Ginger Jacobs, Rabbi "Jake" Jackofsky, Susan Jaffee, Sally Karlin, Harriet Katz, Barbara Kaufman, Dr. Harold Koenig, Herb Leiman, Marlene Levinson, Norma Levitt, Alvin Lubov, Rabbi Shelly Marder (CCAR), Rabbi Janet Marder (CCAR), Ben Mendel, Larry Myers, David Napell, Ross Perloe, Steve Picheny, Dr. Mort Prager, Connie Reiter, Walli Richardson, Eileen Rodgers, Simon Rosenblatt, Selma Sage, Rabbi Sharon Sobel, Ted Ruskin, Esther Saritsky, Dr. Aaron Scholnik, Norman Shubert, Larry Simon, Margie Somers, Bonnie Steinberg, David Toomim, Joan Wachstein, Arlene Weintraub, Ann Wenger, Aggie Zarkadis, and Dr. Walter Zukoff. Likewise, we are thankful for the participation of the North American Federation of Temple Brotherhoods through Jon Shallett and the Women of Reform Judaism through Cindee Gold, Marcia Rosenstein, Carolyn Kunin, and Shelly Lindauer. The Sacred Aging Committee is part of the Department of Jewish Family Concerns, whose board is so ably led by Jean Abarbanel and assisted by vice-chairs Linda Wimmer and Mike Grunebaum.

The support of the leadership of the Union for Reform Judaism is also deeply appreciated. Rabbi Eric Yoffie, president of the Union, and Robert Heller, the URJ Board chair, have encouraged this project, and Rabbi Elliott Kleinman, director of program, helped ensure its continued growth. Of course, the success of this book would never have been realized without the talent and patience of Rabbi Hara Person, Michael Goldberg, and the rest of the staff of the URJ Press. In addition we thank the members of the classes at

Hebrew Union College–Jewish Institute of Religion in New York who were part of pilot classes on sacred aging during the 2004–2005 academic year.

Finally, and with great affection and respect, special thanks for their continuing support to the Jewish Family Concerns "family": Rabbi Edie Mencher, assistant director; Lynn Levy, program coordinator and director of the Aleph-Bet of Marriage program; and Aylah Cohen, our administrative assistant. The movement is blessed to have such dedicated staff.

Rabbi Richard F. Address, D.Min.
Director, URJ Department of Jewish Family Concerns

Introduction

There is a wonderful text in Deuteronomy that speaks of the death of Moses. The text teaches us that Moses died with his "eyes undimmed" and his "vigor unabated" (Deuteronomy 34:7). Why do we look at this text to introduce a resource and program guide on sacred aging? Because the text reveals to us a significant message for how we, at the beginning of the twenty-first century, should embrace the revolution in longevity that is now unfolding. We are taught that personal and spiritual growth are a part of our engagement with life and that relationships should be affirmed as long as we have breath. Aging is potentially a stage that allows us to unwrap the gifts of life that often go unused. New insights, new opportunities to learn, and new opportunities to serve our fellow human beings are presented to an ever-increasing number of us for ever-increasing years. Sacred aging is that component of our growth that places our own lives in a context of history, embraces and celebrates the sacred, and allows us to see ourselves as part of something beyond just our own self.

The Sacred Aging project of the Department of Jewish Family Concerns of the Union for Reform Judaism (URJ) was created as a result of programming focused on older adults within URJ congregations and regions. Over several years of work, we began to see the not-so-subtle demographics that were emerging within our congregations and within the general Jewish community. As part of the department's work in creating the Aleph-Bet of Marriage project, we looked at the major demographic studies within the Jewish community for North America from 1990 through the beginning of the first decade of the twenty-first century. One of the major trends detected was the growth in the older adult population. In the middle of the first decade of the twenty-first century, Jews over the age of sixty-five constitute close to 20 percent of our community, with those over seventy-five making up the greatest growth area within this cohort. What adds to this "revolution" are the members of the baby boom generation, now approaching their sixth decade of life and poised to bring their unique cultural and social history to the area of aging. Thus, within our community we are now experiencing a true revolution of longevity. For many Reform congregations it is no longer unusual that the majority of their membership is over fifty years of age. This new multigenerational cohort represents the longest living, healthiest, most educated, most affluent, and most spiritually challenging generations of older adults that have ever existed within Jewish history. These individuals are destroying myths of what it means to grow older and will continue to develop new forms of families and relationships to each other and to their Judaism. How we as a synagogue movement choose to respond to this new revolution will go a long way in helping to shape the type of Jewish community that evolves in this century. For many in this new world, age has literally become "just a number." We are seeing before us the fluid nature of concepts such as retirement and leisure, the redefinition of work, and the challenge of finding a sense of meaning and purpose. Medical technology, the impact of modern secular culture, and economic and social stability have combined to create a sense of freedom and independence that is changing the face of contemporary older adults. These are truly exciting and challenging times for the Jewish community regarding how it relates to this new longevity revolution. For synagogues, it will mean that everything from programming to cultural attitudes to allocation of both human and financial resources will need to be reassessed. The danger in not doing so, as many are now observing, is that many of our people will just leave. Yet what is important to remember is that our people crave community and relationship. Thus we observe the growing phenomenon of the young old moving into active adult communities throughout North America and seeking to establish contact with other Jewish people. This is giving rise to a slow development of new forms of synagogues within these and associated institutions like assisted-living and life-care facilities.

As the life span extends, we are faced with life stages that are new or are redefined. Just as the "teenager" was an invention of American culture in the twentieth century, we expect that the elder will emerge as a distinct life stage in the twenty-first century. However, a teenager remains one for a defined amount of time; the new older adult culture may last not one decade, but two or three or four. How will the synagogue and the Jewish organizational community respond to this longevity revolution? How will they support, care for, and nurture the new experiences and new life stages that the new majority will experience? Failure to respond in a caring and supportive manner to this new reality may render the synagogue irrelevant to many of this new multigenerational cohort of older Jewish adults. Thus, we are seeing the gradual rise in the creation of and request for new rituals, blessings, and prayers that enhance and support longevity and the desire to see meaning and purpose in that longevity from a spiritual perspective. Likewise, we are witnessing the unfolding of a more "personal" or individual styled Judaism as affiliations with and allegiances to traditional types of communities and institutions fray and lose value.

The Sacred Aging project has been created to raise awareness of the dramatic change within our community regarding the face and dynamic potential of aging. In 2004 and 2005, many congregations piloted a variety of programs that sought to re-vision the culture of aging within the congregation. A series of congregation-based workshops, as well as sessions at URJ regional conventions and meetings, helped explore the impact of this new revolution on congregational life. Additional programs and discussions with Jewish community centers, Jewish family services, and other Jewish organizations and seminaries helped develop how these ideas would be played out in the field.

The project evolved into six categories of programming. These categories represent the six major chapters of this resource book. The contents of the book reflect programs and resources that have been submitted by our pilot sites, as well as material developed by the Department of Jewish Family Concerns for work in the area of spirituality and aging. The first chapter looks at the desire to change the culture of leadership regarding how congregational leadership may view its older adult population. To that end we have included a collection of text-based study scenarios that may be used as discussion starters or triggers at a board meeting or committee meeting. These have been developed to try to raise awareness on the part of leadership regarding the potential of older adult membership and the need to rethink how and why this population can be served. We have also included additional material that provides examples of assessment tools of congregational older adult programming and involvement. This is based on our work in developing years of Caring

Community programs that showed us that boards of trustees and leadership rarely "know" the details of who their members actually are. Since congregations change every four to five years, it is essential that leaders develop ways in which they can understand these changes and thus be proactive in responding to new challenges.

In the development of this project, what continually emerged was the underutilization of the older adult population. By that we mean the reality that this new multigenerational cohort possesses untapped life experience. These are people who built businesses, were and are professionals, lived through the greatest period of change in American history, and have much to teach. This *spiritual capital*, as we call it, needs to be tapped and brought into the life of the congregation. Through mentoring programs, adopt-a-grandparent programs, teaching younger members life skills, or celebrating their stories and journeys, this is powerful human and spiritual material that, we have found, is looking to be involved in meaningful and purposeful ways within the life of the community.

The second chapter will deal with a reality that impacts every congregation. The issue of caregiving is no longer an isolated issue. Indeed, we teach that the "caregiver" is now a new life stage, a stage that is thrust upon an individual and family, and a stage that can last for years. It is a stage that creates stresses and strains within a family, and often those stresses and strains find their way into how people relate to and behave within a congregation. For years we heard tales of people living in the "sandwich generation." What we have learned in developing this project is that today this is more likely to be a "club sandwich." In other words, it is no longer unusual for people to be involved in multigenerational caregiving; for a sixty-year-old man or woman to be caring for his or her eighty-something parent while also caring for his or her thirty-something child and, if geography allows, driving car pool for his or her eight-year-old grandchild.

For years, hundreds of congregations, through their Caring Community programs, have helped ease those caregiving burdens. Yet, as many of us know, much of that caregiving is done in isolation. Women do much of it, and distance is no barometer of ability or willingness to be the designated caregiver. We have encouraged congregations to celebrate the caregivers within their congregations. We have asked that a special service be created to honor those who care and that they be honored as *shomrim*, people who take care of others. In this resource book you will find examples of such liturgies and programs that have begun to be developed. Likewise, you will find additional resources for programming for developing such a caregiver support culture within your community. The Union's *That You May Live Long* (URJ Press) and accompanying study guide can form a basic text for congregations who wish to begin a text-based approach to this subject.

As we began to develop the aspects of the Sacred Aging project, one of the most interesting results was the desire to have congregations and the Reform Movement create rituals and blessings that spoke to new experiences associated with longevity. In a series of ritual creation sessions that the Department of Jewish Family Concerns sponsored in recent years, we received requests for dozens of ideas. Some of these blessings already exist within the context of Jewish tradition. We have just not done a good enough job of teaching them. For example, in every ritual creation workshop there was always the desire for blessings that would celebrate the passage through difficult surgery or treatments. The traditional *Birkat HaGomeil* blessing fits this description perfectly and is available again in *Mishkan T'filah*, the forthcoming prayer book from the Central Conference of American Rabbis. Likewise, there were expected requests for blessings that celebrated grandchildren, retirement, and life transitions into older adulthood. Many of these exist in previous publications and collections of prayers.

What really began to spark our curiosity were requests for new types of blessings. The first was one from a rabbi who asked about the existence of a brief reading that could be done in the sanctuary by a man whose wife had died and who had completed the year of mourning. The congregant's request was for a prayer that would be said as he removed from his finger the wedding ring from his marriage. The rabbi and his congregant created such a prayer, and it is included in our chapter on new rituals. In that chapter you will also find examples of new rituals for new life stages. We are particularly interested in the development of rituals for older adult cohabitation, some of which we have printed here. This issue has raised significant interest and some controversy. In a related vein, we have also included a discussion on another uncomfortable but real situation. We are now seeing an increase in cases where people are dealing with a spouse institutionalized with Alzheimer's disease. In every workshop that we have sponsored in the development of the Sacred Aging project, we dealt with the scenario of the healthy spouse seeking emotional and/or physical comfort from another person, thus raising the question of the need to address this reality and perhaps, in light of this new reality, revisit on a case-by-case basis the very concept of adultery.

No discussion regarding contemporary issues of aging can be complete without including some conversation about the impact of medical technology, perhaps the greatest gift to the fact of longevity. There is no need here to list the accomplishments of medical science and what it has allowed us to do. Indeed, the argument can be made that there would be no longevity revolution had it not been for the advances in medicine and health care in the last several decades. And the horizon is unlimited. With that progress comes additional responsibility for the choices now open to us and often, more complex consequences. How do we seek guidance from Jewish texts and tradition in making sacred decisions in light of emerging medical technology? Our chapter on this subject includes an outline, drawn from Jewish texts, that can be adapted to educational programs within the congregation. The Union's book on decision making and advance directives, *A Time to Prepare* (URJ Press), serves as an existing text to assist congregations in negotiating this difficult but important topic.

The coming years will yield important opportunities for congregations to look at the ethical and public policy issues associated with aging. Medical technology may very soon make it possible for us to match Moses' 120 years of life. The ethical issues associated with that progress need to occupy some of our discussion. Just because we are able to do something does not necessarily mean that we should. These discussions lead to the necessity of engaging our membership in programs that look at how Jewish values impact the subject of health care access and entitlements. Indeed, we need to make sure that these discussions take place on a regular basis within each congregation, as the need for an informed and educated population has never been more evident.

The fifth chapter of this book will look at a more personal aspect of the Sacred Aging project. Part of what we have discovered in our pilot programs is the immense wealth of life experience and creativity that exist within our aging population. We have encouraged congregations to develop "spiritual autobiography" programs that use Jewish texts as a basis for writing or legacy programs that seek to link individuals' search for meaning and purpose to the role that Judaism and Jewish experiences have played within their lives. This section also looks at how we can engage the vast resources of "spiritual capital" that so often go untapped within our congregations. As the members of the baby boom generation age and bring their wealth of life experiences and education to the arena of aging, we need to be prepared to invite into our programs their experience and expertise.

These personal-oriented projects led to the development of congregation-based educational programs that focus on the spiritual and familial needs and lives of our growing older population. The sixth chapter of the book illustrates a variety of educational programs that speak to the issues of the longevity generation. These programs are examples of events that have been successful and ideas for programs that need to be tried. We have included ideas that will not cost a congregation a penny as well as ideas that will require funding. We have included a look at how you may model a project that develops new congregational forms within assisted-living facilities, as well as how we can be mindful of the needs of our older gay, lesbian, bisexual, and transgender members. We encourage individual congregations, clusters of congregations, or regions to move forward in the development of similar programs that enable the new Jewish older adults to find meaning and purpose that are rooted in Jewish texts and traditions and are supported by their congregational family.

In the development of the Sacred Aging project, we have learned many things. We have been energized by the enthusiasm that members of congregations have shown as they dialogued with us. We have been supported by the reality that there is a growing need for our community and our congregations to affirm the power and potential that exist within the multigenerational aging population. We have also learned the necessity of creating a foundation for our work from sacred texts, which speak to the realities of aging in ways that continue to be revealed. The texts support the fundamental reality for all of us that we stand in relationship with God and that the most important need we have is to create relationships with others, hopefully modeling our fundamental relationship with God. That basic need to be with others relates to the reality that is gradually present as we age, the reality of our own mortality. With that reality comes our search to find meaning and purpose in our own lives. In that search we then come to understand that Judaism teaches valuable life lessons as we age; we appreciate the value of being open to change, of accepting new possibilities, and of making life choices that embrace holiness and celebrate life. To honor and respect our elders is to do the same for ourselves and to stand in sacred relationship with God. This is our calling, and we invite you to become a part of what is now a revolution in longevity, spirituality, life, and love.

Responding to the Longevity Revolution: A Guide for Leaders

One who greets an elder is as though he has greeted the face of the Shechinah.
B'reishit Rabbah 63:6

This chapter will address the following needs:

• Assessing the needs of the changing membership through Jewish text study and discussion guides for congregational leaders
• Assessing the needs, interests, and demographics of the changing congregational membership

There is an insightful passage from the midrash that proclaims that "some people have years, while others have old age." Take a look at the current Jewish older adult population and you can see just how prophetic is this centuries-old passage. The current generation of Jewish older adults represents a group that is unique in the annals of Jewish history. Never before have so many lived so long and so well.

This is truly the first generation to benefit from the dramatic and continuing progress being made in the field of health care. In ever-increasing numbers, older adults have discovered what many scholars call life's "third stage." This has allowed them to be in a position not only to give the gift of their own life experience, but also to be open to receive the gifts of Jewish tradition informed by that life experience.

Population studies of the Jewish community that were done in the early 1990s began to create the portrait of this evolving community. Studies completed at the beginning of the twenty-first century continued to see this "trend to older" reflected in an emerging older community that was more "American" than ever.[1] According to these studies, this is a population that is more affluent and mobile than at any other time in Jewish history. It is a pop-

---

1. For instance, the majority of the current older adult population is American-born, as compared to a 1970 survey, which saw 60 percent as immigrants.

ulation that is on the move, often spending two months or more away from a primary residence. Likewise, it is a Jewish population that is redefining the nature of the family in that the majority of the members of this group live in one- or two-person households. The "longevity generation" is really multilayered. Currently, close to 20 percent of our community is sixty-five years of age or older. By 2010, the first wave of the baby boom generation will turn sixty-five. Bringing their own generational "baggage" to the issue of aging, they will swell the ranks of older adults to new and challenging levels. Decades ago the generations may have been at "war" over issues such as Vietnam, civil rights, Watergate, music, and culture; now, they stand to be united on issues concerning caregiving, end-of-life challenges, entitlement programs, and health care. How we as a synagogue community reach out to, embrace, and support this new revolution will go a long way in determining the type of Jewish community we create.

The booming population of older adults will force us to reorganize how synagogues address the needs of this generation. Understanding the population shift in all of its dynamic nuances—such as the activities they engage in, the types of assistance they need physically, and their spiritual aspirations—is paramount to creating a "caring community" within a congregation. Congregations must reexamine personal meaning, leisure, health care, economics, and the definition of family, sexuality, and political power in catering to this expanding older population.

How do these older congregants relate to the changing dynamics within synagogue life? How do they think in terms of membership in Jewish organizations, human resources, mobility, finances, and the need to create new and meaningful responses to an ever-expanding life? The current older adult population is forcing the organized Jewish community to address the question of how that community sees the older Jew. Congregations cannot afford to misinterpret or ignore the needs of this aging generation, or else they risk discontent, frustration, and disconnection to a vital group of congregants. The empowerment of the new Jewish older adult will demand that our synagogues, organizations, and agencies focus upon the desires and needs of its aging members. We know that the nature of synagogue life is changing. *If we do not see the challenges and opportunities for our congregations inherent in the new Jewish older adult, this growing population will see the synagogue as nothing more than a place for life-cycle ceremonies and not as a sacred community of meaning.*

Perhaps the greatest need today is for Jewish organizations to understand the spiritual needs of their aging constituents. The most telling question for the older population today is, "In what ways can I live so as to give my life meaning?" The need and the search for the sacred in life define much of the older adult life. The aging generation is aware of a sense of mystery that infuses life and an acceptance of the power of that mystery to influence life.

How can we begin to understand what this generation of older adults needs or wants? Where do congregations begin to build a community that caters to the spiritual revolution that currently is upon us? Only through careful planning and thoughtful steps can a Jewish organization hope to address this generation. It would be a serious mistake to simply try to develop Jewish programming ideas for older adults without first understanding their spiritual, physical, and mental needs.

Two preliminary steps, therefore, should be taken before any congregation can begin to build a successful "caring community." Both steps are designed to begin the discussion of how we, as a caring congregation, can examine the needs of the aging population in a spiritually fulfilling way that is respectful of the wealth of wisdom and experience the older population possesses. The first is through the study of Jewish **texts**, and the second is by formulating thoughtful **assessment tools** that analyze the physical and spiritual needs of the older population, as well as the capabilities of congregations to meet those needs.

Jewish Text Study

According to the Rabbis, among all the deeds that will earn a person a place in the world-to-come, the study of Torah equals them all (*Mishnah Penah* 1:1; Babylonian Talmud, *Shabbat* 127a). Both ancient and modern texts play an important role in Judaism. Our tradition, rich with wisdom and scholarship, invites us to utilize the teachings of our ancestors in addressing modern needs. In confronting the concerns of our aging communities, congregational leaders may want to use texts to better understand how Judaism addresses the aging populace, to enhance the spirituality of their programs, and to help the community better understand how they can assist the aging population.

Studying Jewish texts prompts us to face certain issues. By studying our tradition, we learn that we are not the only ones to have faced concerns about growing older. Additionally, studying Jewish texts forces us to share our feelings and concerns as we learn from each other what makes us joyful and what makes us apprehensive about what the future may bring.

Following are a few examples of Jewish texts that each deal differently with the aging and caregiving process. Each text is relevant to the sacred aging of the elders within our community in a different way. For example, whereas one text may address the hardships encountered by caregivers in trying to care for their elders, another may concentrate on the joys and moments of happiness that older people feel during the third stage of their lives.

Clergy do not have to be the only ones to lead a text study group. Our tradition supports lay leaders who want to take it upon themselves to both learn and teach from our Jewish sources. Jewish text study provides an opportunity to build relationships among ourselves: "As people talk and share, they learn and understand each other in deeper, more meaningful ways. Texts promote Jewish values and deeper understanding of why helping others and building community deepens each person spiritually. Through doing and through learning the meaning behind what you do, you and your community create sacred space."[2]

Learning Torah refers to much more than just the Five Books of Moses. It includes all of the expansive Jewish literature created by our ancestors, both ancient and modern. The study of Torah connects us to the feelings and needs of others. It also brings us closer to God. In this way, studying Torah becomes a spiritual process, allowing us to create deeper friendships with each other. Simply stated, it makes us holy.

Irrespective of whether you have led Torah study groups, have participated in them, or are new to the process, think of Jewish textual study as an introduction to understanding the wishes, desires, and joys of the aging population. Before one can begin to create meaningful programming ideas within a congregation, it is incumbent upon the group to first understand on a spiritual level what those needs are. Torah study brings those needs to light.

---

2. Harriet Rosen, "A Guide for Lay-Led Text Study," *Becoming a Kehillat Chesed: Creating and Sustaining a Caring Congregation* (New York: URJ Press, 2005), p. 35. We recommend this publication for any congregation that wants to start a caring community to address the needs of the older population. *Becoming a Kehillat Chesed* is available for purchase from the URJ Press, **www.urjpress.com**.

Once we have illuminated the thoughts, misgivings, apprehensions, and joys of both caregivers and elders alike, we can then approach the subject of how congregations can create meaningful programs designed to address those needs.

It is always a good idea to begin each text study session with the blessing for Torah study. The blessing for Torah study commands that each one of us actually become actively engaged with the text. By engaging ourselves in the text, we engage each other and, hopefully, set our minds to the task of better understanding each other's needs.

בָּרוּךְ אַתָּה יְיָ אֱלֹהֵינוּ מֶלֶךְ הָעוֹלָם אֲשֶׁר קִדְּשָׁנוּ בְּמִצְוֹתָיו וְצִוָּנוּ לַעֲסוֹק בְּדִבְרֵי תוֹרָה.

Baruch atah Adonai, Eloheinu Melech haolam, asher kid'shanu b'mitzvotav
v'tzivanu laasok b'divrei Torah.

Blessed are You, Eternal our God, Sovereign of the universe, who has sanctified us through Your commandments and commanded us to engage in the study of Torah.

The following thirty-minute exercises may be used to open a meeting of an organizing committee or a group of laypersons who are developing caring community programs for older persons. The facilitator[3] should begin the session by handing out copies of the following scenarios and having one person read them out loud to the rest of the group. Alternatively, the group can break up into small groups (called *chevruta*) of two or three to read and discuss each text, coming together in the end to summarize what they have discovered.

Text Study A. Positive Healthy Aging

This text deals with the issue of healthy aging: how can communities better assess the needs and concerns of the aging populace?

Scenario

You are a board member who has in the past been very active in the congregation's adult education and programming committees. A past president comes to you. He is upset because although he has tried on his own through the past few years, he has been unable to develop any programs within the synagogue that address the needs of older persons. The president himself is approaching seventy years of age. The past president notes that although the synagogue membership includes a great number of young families and singles, the congregation will soon reach a stage where the majority of its members will be over the age of sixty-five.

After considering his words, you have asked for and gained permission to begin a committee at your synagogue. This is the first meeting, the goal of which is to better understand the needs, anxieties, and desires of the aging population within the synagogue's membership.

Have each group read the following text passage and then address the questions that follow.

---

3. This book is designed to give clergy, lay leaders, caregivers, and elderly congregants alike the tools necessary to create a sustaining and meaningful caring community within their Jewish organization. Accordingly, we hope that the reader will not think that when the term "clergy" is used, it is meant to suggest that only rabbis or cantors are capable of performing a certain task. Likewise, it should not be supposed that the term "lay person" means that clergy are exempted from the topic being discussed. The authors will leave it to the various participants involved in creating and sustaining a caring community to determine who is more or less capable of carrying out a certain function.

Text

The Physician's Prayer

Supreme God in heaven: before I begin my holy work, to heal the human beings whom Your hands formed, I pour out my entreaty before Your throne of glory, that You grant me the strength of spirit and great courage to do my work faithfully, and that the ambition to amass riches or goodness shall not blind my eyes from seeing rightly. Give me the merit to regard every suffering person who comes to ask my advice as a human being, without any distinction between rich and poor, friend and foe, good person and bad. When a person is in distress, show me only the human being. If physicians with greater understanding than mine wish to teach me understanding, then give me the desire to learn from them because there is no limit to the learning of medicine. But when fools insult me, I pray, let my love of the profession strengthen my spirit without any regard for the advanced age of the scorning and their prestige. Let the truth alone be a lamp to my feet, for every yielding in my profession can lead to perdition or illness for a human being whom Your hands formed. I pray You, compassionate and gracious God, strengthen and fortify my body and soul, and implant an intact spirit within me.

Maimonides

Study Questions

1. What do we learn from this text about caring for and valuing the aged?
2. What kind of "spirit and great courage" is needed to help the aging population?
3. This prayer is called "The Physician's Prayer." Why should it be studied by a group of nonphysicians who are interested in aiding older persons? What relevance does it have to our purpose?
4. What does Maimonides mean when he says, "When a person is in distress, show me only the human being"?
5. What kind of distresses could the older persons in our community be experiencing? Does this prayer stress mostly their physical, spiritual, or mental needs?
6. Maimonides talks about how his efforts in trying to help someone can lead to "perdition or illness." What does he mean by this? In trying to help the aging population within our community, how can our own efforts lead to "perdition or illness"?

After each group discusses these questions for about ten to fifteen minutes, the facilitator should ask the groups to highlight what they have discussed. At the end of the exercise, the leader should mention that by studying this text as an opening to the meeting, it is hoped that everyone has a better understanding of what is meant by caring for another human being.

Additional Texts

Some people have years, and others have old age.

B'reishit Rabbah 59:6

He used to say, "At five [one begins the study of] Bible. At ten the Mishnah. At thirteen [one takes on] the [responsibility for] the mitzvot. At fifteen [one begins the study of] the Talmud. At eighteen [one is ready for] marriage. At twenty to pursue [a livelihood]. At thirty [one attains full] strength. At forty [one gains] understanding. At fifty [one gives] counsel. At sixty [one reaches] old age. At seventy [one reaches] the fullness of age. At eighty [one reaches] strong old age. At ninety [one is] bent. And, at one hundred, it is as if one had already died and passed from the world."

Pirkei Avot 5:21

Rav Adda bar Ahavah asked him: To what do you attribute your longevity? He replied: I have never displayed any impatience in my house, and I have never walked in front of any man greater than myself, nor have I ever meditated over Torah in any dirty alleys, nor have I ever walked four cubits without musing over torah or without wearing *t'fillin*, nor have I ever fallen asleep in the synagogue for any length of time or even momentarily, nor have I rejoiced at the disgrace of my friends, nor have I ever called my neighbor by a nickname given to him.

Babylonian Talmud, *Taanit* 20b

Human being is a disclosure of the divine. The grandeur of human being is revealed in the power of being human.

Abraham J. Heschel, *The Insecurity of Freedom: Essays on Human Existence* (New York: Schocken Books, 1972), p. 25

Text Study B. Alienation

This text addresses the loneliness and alienation that some people may feel as they grow older. How can a person cope with the loss of a loved one or the potential death of a good friend?

Scenario

Judy and Millie have been best friends for many years. Together they have watched their children grow, celebrated family holidays, and vacationed with each other.

But then life suddenly and abruptly changed for both of them. Judy lost her husband to cancer, and Millie suddenly contracted cancer herself. She has been in and out of remission for a few years, and Millie's struggle has been enormous.

The two women talk every day. Their optimism grows with the support that they receive from each other. Nevertheless, the death of Judy's husband and Millie's serious illness weigh heavily on their minds.

Texts

Moses was 120 years old when he died; his eyes were undimmed and his vigor unabated. And the Israelites bewailed Moses in the steppes of Moab for thirty days.

Deuteronomy 34:7–8

A young tree bends; an old tree breaks.

Yiddish proverb

Study Questions

1. What does it mean to have eyes that are undimmed and vigor that is unabated? Is this to be taken literally or metaphorically?
2. Why is it important for the Torah to tell us how old Moses was when he died? Does age affect one's ability to enjoy life?
3. How can Millie and Judy use these texts as positive reinforcement for the travails that they have experienced?
4. How does the Yiddish proverb differ from the quote from Deuteronomy?

Additional Texts

Cast me not off in the time of my old age; when my strength fails, forsake me not.

Psalm 71:9

It is easy to criticize others and make them feel unwanted. Anyone can do it. What takes effort and skill is picking them up and making them feel good.

Nachman of Bratzlav

Rabbi Hillel taught, "Do not separate yourself from the community" (*Pirkei Avot* 2:4). Mitzvot bring the individual into the context of community. As we have seen, performing mitzvot provides us with another prism through which the spiritual life can be evaluated. Through the fulfillment of mitzvot, particularly those *bein adam lachaveiro* (between individuals), we are brought closer to God. That's one of the many reasons why Rabbi Y'hoshua ben Korcha taught, "One should always be as alert as possible to perform a mitzvah" (Babylonian Talmud, *Nazir* 23b).

Why is the story of Abraham's circumcision followed by the visitation of God? God came to visit while Abraham was recuperating, to make clear the mitzvah of visiting the sick.

Babylonian Talmud, *Bava M'tzia* 86b

Text Study C. Valuing Experience

Whether the message is positive or negative, we can all learn from the lives of each other. As we grow older, we learn to appreciate the wisdom and experience that we have collected over the years. The following texts teach us how can we learn from the experience gained from our elders.

Scenario

Jack has always had a terrific relationship with his mother, Adele. As Adele grew older, Jack swore that he would use all of his financial means to care for and support his mother.

As Adele approached her mid-seventies, Jack noticed that she was having a harder time living on her own. So with Jack's invitation, his mother came to live with Jack and his family.

After a few years, though, it was apparent that Adele needed more help than Jack could give. One day, Adele fell and fractured her hip. Adele's doctors and Jack's friends repeatedly tried to convince Jack that his mother should be in a nursing home, where she would receive more attention.

Adele cried when her son suggested that she live in a nearby nursing home. Of course, Jack was devastated with guilt. He thought to himself: How can I do such a thing to my mother? After all she has done for me, is it fair to kick her out of my house?

Texts

Honor your father and your mother, that you may long endure on the land that the Eternal your God is assigning to you.

Exodus 20:12

You shall each revere your mother and your father.

Leviticus 19:3

Study Questions

1. What is the difference between "honoring" and "revering" your parents?
2. In what sense do these passages bestow a sense of obligation upon us? As children, what exactly are our obligations toward our parents?
3. If Adele continues to refuse to be placed in a home, will Jack be "dishonoring" her by insisting that she move?
4. What does it mean for a person to "long endure on the land"?
5. Why does the Exodus passage mention God? How does invoking God's name help us to honor or revere our parents?

Additional Texts

Birth is a beginning, and death a destination. And life is a journey: from childhood to maturity, and youth to age; from innocence to awareness, and ignorance to knowing; from foolishness to discretion, and then, perhaps, to wisdom.

Alvin Fine

You shall rise before the aged and show deference to the old.

Leviticus 19:32

The glory of youth is in their strength. The majesty of the old is in their gray hairs.

Proverbs 20:29

There is no reason in old men, and no counsel in children!

Babylonian Talmud, *Shabbat* 89b

Show respect to an old man who has forgotten his learning through no fault of his own, for we have learned that the fragments of the old tablets were kept alongside the new tablets in the Ark of the Covenant.

Babylonian Talmud, *B'rachot* 8b

Perhaps this is the most urgent task: to save the inner man from oblivion, to remind ourselves that we are a duality of the mysterious grandeur and the pompous dust. Our future depends upon our appreciation of the reality of the inner life, of the splendor of thoughts, of the dignity and wonder of reverence. This is the most important thought: God has a stake in the life of man, of every man. But this idea cannot be imposed from without; every man must discover it; it cannot be preached, it must be experienced.

Abraham J. Heschel, *The Insecurity of Freedom:*
Essays on Human Existence, pp. 12–13

You should not look at all the bad things in your life and say, "Now I will improve myself." Rather you should look at your positive traits that you have gained and dwell upon your goodness. From there you can say, "Now I will prove myself."

Nachman of Bratzlav

Text Study D. Individual Growth

The following texts can be used to explore the issue of individual growth. What is the difference between being "young" and "old"? What new things can a person experience in the later years of life?

Scenario

Ed and his wife, Denise, have had a wonderful life together. Although they started having children a bit later in life, they raised three adorable and loving children. Ed and Denise have watched their children grow from being toddlers, to becoming teenagers, and finally into young adulthood.

Lately, however, Ed has been feeling nostalgic about his life. The upcoming high school graduation of his youngest daughter, Amelia, has made him even more reflective than usual. Ed has been feeling sad about seeing his youngest child leaving home for college, even though Amelia is a promising young woman who undoubtedly will have a successful college career.

Ed is now at the traditional age of retirement. As Amelia's high school graduation approaches, Ed feels the need to tell Amelia the various lessons he has learned throughout his lifetime. He wants to let Amelia know that although he is approaching retirement, he still feels young in both his heart and his mind. He wants to impart to Amelia how different his mind works now from when he was entering college. Ed's mind begins to swirl with a multitude of lifetime lessons that he wants to impart to Amelia on the difference between his life as a young man and his life today.

Knowing how her husband has been feeling lately, on the morning of Amelia's graduation, Denise hands Ed the following excerpt from *Pirkei Avot* (Teachings of the Fathers).

Text

Elisha ben Abuyah said, "Regarding the one who studies when young, to what can that person be compared? To ink written on new paper. Regarding the one who studies when old, to what can that person be compared? To ink written on paper that has been erased." Rabbi Yosei ben Y'hudah of K'far HaBavli said, "Regarding the one who learns from the young, to what can this person be compared? To one eating unripe grapes and drinking wine from the winepress. Regarding the person who learns from the old, to what can this person be compared? To one eating ripe grapes and drinking old wine." Rabbi, however, said, "Don't look at the wine flask, but rather at what is in it. For there are new wine flasks filled with old wine, and there are old wine flasks that don't even have new wine."

Pirkei Avot 4:20

Study Questions

1. What is the difference between what Elisha ben Abuyah says and what Yosei ben Y'hudah says? How do they each treat the issue of being young as opposed to being old?
2. What is the metaphor of the wine flask that Rabbi alludes to supposed to mean? How does this metaphor either support or contradict what his two colleagues have said?
3. Rabbi Yosei ben Y'hudah talks about learning from the "old" and learning from the "young." Is he using these two terms literally or metaphorically? Do you know people who are young in age, but old in wisdom?
4. If you were Ed, what do you think you would tell your daughter after reading this text? How could you use this text to spark a conversation with your own children or grandchildren?

Additional Texts

"All right," he whispered, "now here's the payoff. Here is how we are different from these wonderful plants and animals. As long as we can love each other, and remember the feeling of love we had, we can die without ever really going away. All the love you created is still there. All the memories are still there. You live on—in the hearts of everyone you have touched and nurtured while you were here. . . . Death ends a life, not a relationship."

Mitch Albom, *Tuesdays with Morrie* (New York: Doubleday, 1997), pp. 173–174

We are meaning seeking animals. We want to know who we are, what we can know, what we can hope for, why we were born. We seek meaning in the work we pursue, the relationships we forge, the homes we build, and the communities to which we belong. When we form congregations . . . we are really seeking meaning. Wherever and however we seek meaning in life, whether in the religious or secular world, the answers to the questions, "Who am I?" and "Why am I?" define a theology—a special theology that is our own.

Carol Ochs, *Our Lives as Torah: Finding God in our Stories* (Hoboken, NJ: John Wiley & Sons, 2001), p. 2

If people do not plow in the summer, what will they eat in the winter?

Mishlei Rabbah 6

Psalms

Biblical poetry from the Book of Psalms can also be a source of inspiration for both caregivers and the elderly. The following list of psalms, created by Rabbi Gerald Kane of Temple Beth-El in Las Cruces, New Mexico, can be used in a number of ways. Like all religious poetry, psalms can be read simply for spiritual inspiration. In a group setting, however, they can also be a powerful tool to discover the emotions and attitudes of the entire group. We encourage lay leaders to consider these psalms when addressing a particular issue pertaining to caring for the elderly.

Suggested Psalms for Caregivers and the Elderly

Issue	Psalms
Dealing with the stress of aging	4
Feeling discouraged	23, 42
Loneliness	40
Joy, happiness, celebration	97, 99, 100
When grateful for God's gift of life	135
When needing spiritual inspiration	27
Worrying about the future	34
Pain, anguish, discontentment	31, 34
Courage to face new issues	27, 31, 56, 62
Hoping for health[4]	6, 27, 39, 41
When in need of help	121, 130, 146

Further Text Study

There are a myriad of Jewish texts that can be used to assess the needs of caregivers and the aging population alike. For additional text ideas, facilitators should consult *That You May Live Long: Caring for Our Aging Parents, Caring for Ourselves*, edited by Richard F. Address and Hara E. Person (New York: UAHC Press, 2003), and *Becoming a Kehillat Chesed*, referenced earlier. Other areas of interest that facilitators may want to explore include creating a community, focusing on positive change, confidentiality, illness and healing, support for the caregiver, and decision making for the future.

There probably are literally hundreds of categories that pertain to understanding the needs of the aging population and their caregivers. Lay leaders should consult with their clergy to determine what texts best fit any given scenario. Additionally, the use of surveys to assess the particular demographics of any Jewish community will help determine what those needs may be. Asking pointed questions that are designed to elicit meaningful and thoughtful responses will help everyone understand what the aging population expects and wants out of its Jewish organization.

Using Surveys to Assess Needs and Demographics

> Take a census of the whole Israelite company . . .
>
> Numbers 1:2

Studying Jewish texts is only one component of introducing your congregation to the idea of creating a caring community. Practical considerations also must be addressed as a

---

4. Reb Nachman of Bratzlav suggested the following "healing psalms" as an inspiration for one who is sick or infirmed: 16, 32, 41, 42, 59, 77, 90, 105, 137, and 150.

preliminary step to caring for the elderly. Through Jewish texts, we are able to better understand the lives of the individuals in our congregations. However, it is also incumbent upon a congregation to assess the structure of the organic whole.

Before a congregation can know what programs to implement in order to care for its older members, it is necessary for congregational leaders to take certain preliminary steps to understand the general makeup of the entire congregation. Caring for older adults involves preparation. The specific needs and concerns of the aged within the community should be assessed so that the leadership does not waste its time and efforts on programs that will not have any lasting effect.

One way to discover the psychological and physical needs of the older community within a congregation is through the use of surveys. By asking people to describe what they desire from their congregation, congregational leaders will be able to more effectively understand how to provide love and compassion to the aged. Moreover, such survey mechanisms with periodic repetition can be instrumental in helping a congregation anticipate human and programmatic needs for older adults.

Conducting a population survey within a Jewish congregation does not have to be a mundane process. Congregational leaders can, and should, try their best to bring an element of spirituality to the process. The message should be clear: the congregation wants to find out how best to respond to and anticipate the needs, hopes, and dreams of the older adults within their community. Performing a mitzvah by helping another—whether it be by visiting the physically infirm or raising the spirituality level of others—brings one closer to God and adds a sense of holiness to the process. Conducting a survey can unlock the mystery of God's presence in order to provide a reservoir of strength, faith, and spiritual growth. There exists a sacred link between how we go about taking care of our loved ones and our relationship with God. Our texts stress the idea of respecting our loved one's wishes. Using surveys to determine those wishes can also be a holy and spiritual task.

Below are a few samples of the types of questions congregational leaders may wish to use to assess the needs of the aging populace. These examples are presented as models. Good questionnaires start with knowing what kinds of information are being sought and for what purpose the information is being collected. As you begin to approach the exciting possibilities of programming for older adults and their families, your congregation will adapt and innovate these models to best suit your particular needs.

Furthermore, it is important to understand that a survey should not create false hopes. In other words, congregations should first assess their financial capabilities and physical resources before handing out any survey. A survey should be carefully tailored so that it reflects the culture of the congregation and does not create expectations that the congregation is unwilling or unable to fulfill. For guidelines on creating forms that ask questions tailored to your particular congregation's goals, see "Creating Surveys and Assessments," in *Becoming a Kehillat Chesed*, p. 6.

Senior Adult Surveys

Senior Adult Survey A

1. How do you envision your own aging? What is your attitude about it?

2. How does your growing older affect your participation in services, leadership roles, volunteer work, social action, classes and lectures, and intergenerational activities?

3. What are your expectations of:

    a. The professional staff (rabbis, cantors, educators, program director)?

    b. Lay leaders and other congregants?

4. Choose the top five categories of "caring" that you most desire from your congregation:

___ Visits	___ Practical help	___ Holiday observance
___ Phone calls	___ Encouragement	___ Praying with me
___ Respite care	___ Presence	___ Praying for me
___ Support groups	___ Referrals	___ Other (explain below)

5. In what ways can the congregation work on the spiritual and practical issues of aging within the community?

6. Beyond funerals and shivah calls, how can the congregation help its older members with the dying and grieving process?

Senior Adult Survey B[5]

1. Are you male or female?

2. How old are you?

    a. Under 60

    b. 60–70

    c. 70–80

    d. Over 80

3. What is your marital status?

    a. Married

    b. Widow/widower

    c. Divorced

    d. Single

4. What is your living situation?

    a. I live alone.

    b. I live with my spouse/companion.

---

5. Adapted from a survey by Main Line Reform Temple Beth Elohim, Wynnewood, Pennsylvania.

c. I live in an assisted-living facility.

d. I live with my children.

e. Other (please specify): _____

5. What is your primary mode of transportation?

a. I drive and have access to a car.

b. I drive but do not have access to a car.

c. I use public transportation.

d. I rely on friends.

e. I use taxis with my senior discount.

f. Other (please specify): _____

6. What time of the day is good for you to participate in programs at the synagogue?

a. During the day

b. In the evening

7. When would you like to see more programming? (Circle all that apply.)

a. On weekdays during the day

b. On weekdays at night

c. On the weekends during the day

d. On the weekends at night

e. In the summer during the day

f. In the summer at night

g. Other (please specify): _____

8. Are there additional or different religious activities that you would like to see the synagogue offer?

a. Daily minyan

b. Torah study

c. *Chavurah* (a small worship group)

d. Torah readings on Friday night

e. Other (please specify): _____

9. What program length do you prefer?

a. Ongoing for several months

b. Ongoing for several weeks

c. Single programs

d. Other (please specify): _____

10. What types of activities would you like to participate in at the synagogue? (Circle all that apply.)

a. Social activities and educational activities

b. Potluck/covered dish dinner

c. Health education program

d. Book talk

e. Money management information

f. Health insurance information

g. Retirement planning

h. Hospital visits

i. Meals for homebound

j. Transportation

k. Intergenerational work within the congregation

l. Other (please specify): _____

Name (optional): _____

Phone and e-mail (optional): _____

May we contact you for further information and input? Yes _____ No _____

Thank you for your time and assistance in helping us create exciting and worthwhile programming to better serve our community and congregation.

Please return this survey to the main office at the synagogue.

Senior Adult Survey C[6]

Dear Congregant:

Would you like to swing on a star? Carry moonbeams home in a jar?

Nothing quite so drastic, you say? Well, what then? What do you want to do with your time? We'd love to know—because we're your synagogue, and we want to be a greater part of your life!

Please spend a few minutes and fill out this survey to help us plan together for a fun, stimulating future.

What is your birth date? Month _____ Day _____ Year _____

---

6. Adapted from a survey by Temple Israel, Dayton, Ohio.

Are you male _____ or female _____ ?

In what part of town do you live? _____ Do you live there year-round?

      Yes _____ No _____

If not, when are you here? Summer ____ Fall ____ Winter ____ Spring ____ Holidays only ____

Would you like to do more in your spare time? Yes _____ No _____

Do you volunteer? Yes _____ No _____

If yes, please describe your volunteer involvement on a separate page.

What kind of activities do you enjoy? (See below.)

Participate in	Currently	Would like to
Exercise programs		
Nutrition programs		
Friendship groups		
Drama clubs		
Music performances		
Meditation/relaxation programs		
Grandparenting programs		
Square, line, or Israeli dancing		
Ballroom dancing		
Sports		
Cards, mah-jongg, etc.		
Board games		
Volunteer projects		
Other games		
Concerts or theater		
College courses		
Art classes		
Music classes		
Jewish study programs		
Transcultural programs		
Book clubs		
Discussion groups		
Business/professional groups		
Health education programs		
Gourmet cooking		
Day trips out of town		
Gardening classes		
Other		

List organizations to which you currently belong:

When do you see family and/or friends?

  a. Every day

  b. Once a week

  c. Once a month

  d. Holidays only

How do you consider your health?

  a. Excellent

  b. Good

  c. Fair

  d. Poor

Do you have any health problems? Yes _____ No _____
If you would like, please explain (all information will remain confidential).

Please describe the type of assistance you currently receive or need for daily activities:

Service	Currently Use	Need
Transportation		
Meals		
Homemaker/home health aide		
Friendly visitor		
Telephone calls		
Money management		
Health insurance information		
Income tax assistance		
Insurance claims filings		
Retirement planning		
Support group		
Obtaining medication		
Taking medication		

Are you receiving services from an agency? Yes _____ No _____
If yes, please explain:

If you feel comfortable doing so, please share with us your financial situation (all information will remain confidential):

1. How financially stable are you?

2. From where do you receive financial support?

3. What is your monthly disposable income, after taking into consideration all of the activities that you are already engaged in?

4. Do you receive Medicaid/Medicare benefits? Do you have an elder law attorney helping you with your personal finances? If not, would you like one to be recommended to you?

5. Would you benefit from a financial planning program at your congregation?

We need your help! Please share how we can be of help to you.
Comments:

Senior Adult Survey D[7]

Part I—Questions for Older Adults

Are you an older adult (over age 65)? Yes _____ No _____

Please check your age category: 65–70 _____ 70–75 _____ 75–80 _____ Over 80 _____

Do you have family living within thirty miles of your home? Yes _____ No _____

Do you feel your family is available to you in case of emergencies? Yes _____ No _____

Are you able to attend services and synagogue events regularly? Yes _____ No _____

Does your congregation have an older adults club? Yes _____ No _____

---

7. Adapted from Sacred Aging pilot programs in congregations.

Are you currently a member of any of your congregation's committees? Yes _____ No _____

Are you an officer in your congregation? Yes _____ No _____

Would you like to see your congregation offer one or more of the following programs for older adults? Please check all that apply:

_____ Social activities

_____ Day trips

_____ Community service projects

_____ Lecturers/speakers

_____ Entertainment

_____ Lifelong learning programs

_____ Congregational dinners

_____ Torah study

_____ Camping

_____ Travel

_____ Bar/bat mitzvah training

_____ Foster grandparents program

_____ Exercise/fitness program

_____ Day care

_____ Health fair

_____ Healing services

_____ Grief counseling

_____ Caregiver support program

_____ Theater parties

_____ Intergenerational activities

_____ Other (please specify): _____

Would you like to see your congregation publish a newsletter specifically of interest to older adults and their families? Yes _____ No _____

What skills or interests do you have that you can bring to the congregation?

_____ Educational

_____ Entertainment

_____ Administrative

_____ Social

_____ Cultural

_____ Other (please explain)

Part II—Questions for Older Adults and Caregivers[8]

My congregation can help me by providing information about the following:

_____ Transportation

_____ Finances

_____ Opportunities for fun and socializing

_____ Health and nutrition issues

_____ Loneliness

_____ Homemaker services

_____ Moving out of the family home

_____ Telephone reassurance

_____ Making a will

_____ Sexuality in the older adult

_____ Jewish funeral practices

_____ Advance directives/living wills

_____ Making treatment decisions

_____ Religious comfort and support

_____ Fear of old age

_____ Fear of becoming dependent

_____ Emotional alienation from family

_____ Grief counseling

_____ Caregiver support

_____ Widow/widower support

_____ Retirement communities

_____ Nursing homes

_____ Healthy aging

_____ Other: _____

---

8. See chapter 2 for surveys designed to assess the needs of caregivers. Because many of the questions presented here are relevant for both caregivers and those who are in need of care, they have been included in this chapter.

What committees, projects, or special events would you volunteer to be part of in the congregation? Please list some choices.

My congregation can help me best by:

Would you be available to serve on an elder planning committee? Yes _____ No _____

Would you serve on a synagogue committee? Yes _____ No _____

Name and address (optional): _____

_____

_____

Telephone and e-mail: _____

Assessing Resources for Congregational Leaders

Synagogues can be the hub of a rich community life. They can enhance their members' lives by helping to dispel the feelings of isolation and providing support in life crises and its joy in ways that are Jewish and essential in contemporary society. The synagogue is a natural helping network with a pool of knowledge, resources, and competencies, which can be mobilized so the lives of members are strengthened and enriched as they both give and receive.[9]

Assessing the resources that are available for creating a caring community can, and should, be just as spiritually uplifting as assessing the needs of the aging population. Building a relationship within a congregational setting is a holy enterprise unto itself. Torah teaches us to believe in the power of relationships, just as Abraham had faith in God when God commanded Abraham to *lech l'chah*—go forward into another land! Abraham trusted God, and God had earned that trust by promising Abraham a spiritually fulfilling life in the future. The power of individuals working with each other to create sacred communities transforms everyone involved, including the entire structure of the congregation itself. In developing sacred personal relationships and understanding what is needed to accomplish that task, the culture of a congregation is transformed, "one relationship at a time."[10]

---

9. Harriet A. Feiner, "The Synagogue as a Support System" (address to the Jewish Board of Family and Children's Services, New York, n.d.).
10. Harriet Rosen, *Becoming a Kehillat Chesed*, p. ix.

Just as the lay leaders need to know what the needs are of the aging population within their congregation, so too do they need to understand what they are capable of providing in developing a caring community. Surveys and questionnaires can be used by lay leaders and professionals within the congregation to provide a blueprint for the creation of programming ideas. The following are examples of surveys and questionnaires that will guide congregational lay leaders through this process of transforming their institution into a sacred community of caregiving support.

Making Your Synagogue User-Friendly for Older Adults: A Checklist for Congregations[11]

> You shall not insult the deaf, or place a stumbling block before the blind.
> You shall fear your God: I am the Eternal.
>
> Leviticus 19:14

Preparing your congregation for the physical needs of the elderly sends an important message that the congregation genuinely cares about the needs of its aging population. Any Jewish organization that has not already done so should consider assessing whether its physical property is "user-friendly" for the physically challenged. It is the most visible sign that a community sincerely is taking into account the needs of a specific population. Congregants, whether caregivers or the elderly, may enter a building in order to take part in a Jewish programming experience and be inspired by the extra effort the organization has taken to make the building a warm and easily accessible place. If someone's physical body is challenged, then you can expect that it will be all the more difficult to engage them in spiritual mental exercises, such as learning pieces of Jewish text.

The following list is by no means meant to be exhaustive. However, it is a good starting point to try to assess whether your organization's physical premises invites elderly citizens into a warm and caring atmosphere.

1. Do you provide large-type prayer books in the sanctuary and large-type reading materials in the library?
2. Do you provide brighter lighting in the sanctuary?
3. Do you provide optional hearing assistance (infrared, for example)?
4. Do you provide conveniently located and adequate numbers of lavatories? Are restroom doorways and stalls wide enough to accommodate wheelchairs and walkers?
5. Do you use a movable Torah reading table that can be placed on a lower level for readers who cannot walk up steps to the bimah?
6. Do you provide video or audio equipment for recording special events?
7. Is there reserved seating for handicapped or physically challenged older adults?
8. Do you provide outdoor benches for those waiting for a ride? Do you provide a sheltered area for persons getting into and out of automobiles?
9. Have you trained ushers in emergency procedures, such as providing oxygen tanks in an emergency, and utilizing wheelchairs and splints?
10. Are all walkways and uncarpeted areas skid-proof? Have you gotten rid of area rugs, and exposed electrical and telephone cords?

---

11. Created by Lillian Maltzer (*z"l*), UAHC Committee on the Jewish Family.

11. Are all doorways to classrooms, meeting rooms, board rooms, chapel, sanctuary, and lavatories wide enough to accommodate wheelchairs and walkers?

12. When arranging for social activities, conferences, and/or retreats, do you select facilities with elevators to all floors? (Congregations with older buildings that hold functions in a lower level should consider how to make the facility accessible so that all members will be able to participate.)

13. Are your bulletins and newsletters printed in high-contrast ink colors, such as black, dark blue, or burgundy? (Light blue and light gray ink are difficult for visually impaired persons to read.)

Needs Assessment Surveys

These surveys are designed to help lay leaders understand what the congregation both currently requires and will require within the next ten to twenty years. It is important to keep communication open on all levels of the congregational organization. Talk to the clergy at your synagogue, with other board members, and with congregants regarding the questions in these surveys. Again, these surveys are intended as models. Each particular congregation should review all of the surveys to choose one that is most appropriate and revise it according to the particular needs of the congregation.

Needs Assessment Survey A

1. Who are your members? Assess the demographics of your congregation:

   a. Is there a sizable population (at least 15 percent) of members 43 years old or older?

   b. Is there a sizable population (at least 10 percent) of members 65 years old or older?

   c. How many are over 80 years old?

   d. How will these numbers change over the next 5 years? 10 years?

2. What are your goals for older adult programming?

   a. What kinds of programs do your congregants want?

   b. What kinds of programs do your families want and need?

   c. Do you want to increase the participation of older adults in synagogue rituals?

   d. Will you concentrate on providing programs for active seniors?

   e. Do you want to provide supportive services for the elderly who are frail?

   f. What about the families and relatives of older adults?

3. What practical support do your older adults need?

   a. Do you have a resource person on your staff to address the concerns of older adults?

   b. Do you have an older adult committee in your congregation? Will you establish an older adult committee? What age persons will serve on the older adult committee? Will it be intergenerational?

   c. Can you provide transportation to services and other synagogue events?

    d. Do your older adults want and need basic services, visitation, social programs, health and fitness programs, day programs, or recreation programs?

4. Assess your facility:

    a. Is your facility user-friendly? Do you have stairs, large bathrooms, good lighting, and so on?

    b. Do you have emergency medical and first aid supplies readily available?

    c. Will you need to consider remodeling or redesigning the interior or exterior of your buildings?

    d. Can your congregation sustain the expense of upgrading the building to meet federal codes for the disabled? Is the congregation willing to think about this issue?

5. What are the resources that are available in your congregation?

    a. Are there persons in your congregation who would volunteer to serve on a task force to assess and develop programs for older adults? Who are these persons?

    b. How involved are they willing to be in older adult activities?

    c. Have you considered hiring a staff person to coordinate older adult programming and activities?

6. Examine your congregational rituals:

    a. Does your congregation offer services and rituals that celebrate older adults? Do you need to look at new approaches?

    b. Do you have special services for new life-cycle events such as retirement, selling the family home, moving to a smaller home, or moving to a care facility?

    c. Do you provide services for healing, dealing with long-term illness, or loss? Can your congregation's ritual committee get involved?

7. How committed are you?

    a. Why do you want older adult programs and activities for your congregation?

    b. Where will this fit into your congregation's priorities?

    c. What will be the financial commitment from the congregational budget?

    d. Who will develop the action plan and begin to address older adult concerns for your congregation?

    e. Who will coordinate activities?

    f. What do you anticipate to be the ultimate benefit to your congregation? When will you begin to take action?

Needs Assessment Survey B

1. Is your membership composed of one particular age group? Does it cover a broad range or are there several age-group clusters?

2. What are your community's networks?

    a. Are there family units that include grandparents (and great-grandparents) and grand-children within your congregation?

    b. Are there many members who are new to the community?

    c. How many members are without local family or friendship networks?

    d. Are there many members who are alone?

3. In what stages of life are your members?

    ____ Newly married

    ____ Married with children

    ____ Same-sex relationships

    ____ Blended families

    ____ Long-term married

    ____ Widows/widowers

    ____ Twenty/thirty-somethings

    ____ Unmarried

    ____ Divorced

    ____ Empty nesters

    ____ Sandwich generation

    ____ Elderly and alone

4. What specific needs is the board aware of?

    ____ Parent, spouse, or child in need of long-term care

    ____ Disabled adults or children

    ____ A large cluster of recent deaths

    ____ Single-parent households

    ____ Major, long-term chronic or crisis illnesses such as cancer, strokes, HIV/AIDS (to name only a few)

    ____ Loss or traumatic life changes such as divorce or job loss

Needs Assessment Survey C

1. How long have you been affiliated with Temple Shalom?

2. Why did you join Temple Shalom? (Check all that apply.)

    ____ Spirituality

____ Religious school

____ Adult education

____ Size

____ Proximity

____ Long-term family connection

____ Friends at temple

____ Other:

3. What life-cycle events/services have you participated in at Temple Shalom?

____ Bar/bat mitzvah

____ Confirmation

____ Marriage

____ *B'rit*/baby naming

____ Funeral

____ Other:

4. How many people make up your immediate family?

5. What are the ages of the youngest and oldest members of your immediate family?

6. Do you have extended family or close friends living within a two-hour drive from you? Please explain.

7. In which of these ways has the clergy personally assisted your family?

____ Illness

____ Adult education

____ Spiritual guidance

____ Life-cycle counseling (Through which events? Please describe.)

____ Crisis counseling

____ Other:

8. Do you think it is important that Temple Shalom provide programming on local issues? Why or why not?

9. Which groups do you think it is important to support with programs?

____ Youth and teenagers

____ Singles

____ Single parents

____ Gay/lesbian families

____ Intermarried families

____ Seniors

____ Widows/widowers

____ Other:

10. Which of these programs would you attend?

____ Enriching Jewish life

____ Death and bereavement

____ Parent-child relations

____ How to raise Jewish children

____ Empty-nest syndrome

____ Preparing for being a Jewish parent

____ Commitment and marriage

____ Preparation for marriage

____ Other:

11. How do you rate Temple Shalom on the following community responses:

	Never	Seldom	Sometimes	Often	Always
New members are warmly welcomed.	1	2	3	4	5
Our clergy is responsive to individual needs.	1	2	3	4	5
Temple Shalom is a source of new friends.	1	2	3	4	5
Temple Shalom's members respond well to congregants in good and bad times.	1	2	3	4	5

12. How often do you read Temple Shalom's bulletin?

13. Do you read the synagogue mailings about special events? How often?

Name (optional): _____

Would you be willing to speak with someone regarding serving on a committee at Temple Shalom?

What special skills do you have that you may be willing to share with Temple Shalom?

Please add any comments you may have:

These are just a few samples of the types of questions that assess the needs of the community. To further understand how the leadership within a congregation can respond to the changing demographics of the contemporary Jewish family, ask for a copy of "Our Changed Reform Jewish Family: Celebrating a Unity of Diversities" from the URJ Department of Jewish Family Concerns. You can contact them by phone at 212-650-4294, by e-mail at **JFC@urj.org,** or on the Web at **www.urj.org/jfc/.**

Through careful planning, Jewish organizations can begin to understand what is expected of them as our congregants grow older. Every step of the way in creating a caring community should take into consideration the sacredness of the task at hand. No planning should be considered a mundane task, even when it comes to surveying the Jewish population or refitting a physical structure so that it meets the needs of the elderly. Text studies, combined with the use of surveys, are important tools to help caregivers and lay leaders alike understand what is expected of them. Furthermore, these tools help the aging congregants concretize what they want and need, both from a spiritual standpoint and a physical, hands-on standpoint.

Programming for the needs of the elderly is a holy task. But so is planning for that programming. Each step along the path to creating a caring community is an affirmation of our Jewish beliefs. Each step is equally important in fulfilling the mitzvot of honoring our fathers and mothers. Lastly, each step brings us closer to God.

Additional Resources

Books

Berrin, Susan, ed. *A Heart of Wisdom: Making the Jewish Journey from Midlife through the Elder Years.* Woodstock, VT: Jewish Lights Publishing, 1997.

Freeman, David, and Judith Z. Abrams. *Illness and Health in the Jewish Tradition: Writings from the Bible to Today.* Philadelphia: Jewish Publication Society, 1999.

Koenig, Harold G. *Aging and God: Spiritual Pathways to Mental Health in Midlife and Later Years.* Binghamton, NY: Haworth Press, 1994.

Kushner, Harold. S. *The Lord Is My Shepherd: Healing Wisdom of the Twenty-Third Psalm.* New York: Alfred A. Knopf, 2003.

Myerhoff, Barbara. *Number Our Days*. New York: Simon and Schuster, 1978.

Person, Hara E., ed. *The Mitzvah of Healing: An Anthology of Essays, Jewish Texts, Personal Stories, Meditations and Rituals*. New York: UAHC Press, 2003.

Schacter-Shalomi, Zalman, and Ronald S. Miller. *From Age-ing to Sage-ing: A Profound New Vision to Growing Older*. New York: Warner Books, 1997.

Simmons, Henry, and Vivienne S. Pierce. *Pastoral Responses to Older Adults and Their Families: An Annotated Bibliography*. Westport, CT: Greenwood Press, 1992.

Weintraub, Simcha, ed. *Healing of Soul, Healing of Body: Spiritual Leaders Unfold the Strength and Solace in Psalms*. Woodstock, VT: Jewish Lights Publishing, 1994.

Web Sites

www.urj.org/goandstudy/guide/index.shtm: Teaches lay leaders how to study Jewish texts and teach them in group formats.

groups.msn.com/LifeTransitions: Support for families who have placed a loved one in a skilled nursing or similar care facility.

www.aging-religion-spirituality.com: Includes links to a number of important Web sites regarding aging and pastoral care.

www.asaging.org: Educational opportunities and products, links to religious and spiritual groups, health care, lesbian and gay issues, mental health, and multicultural issues.

www.HealingPsalm.com: Teaches groups how to create religious poetry dealing with aging and healing.

www.jewishhealing.org: Includes links to various healing centers and programs.

www.spirituality4aging.org: Explores issues related to spirituality and faith to promote the well-being of older adults.

www.aarp.org/ageline: Includes resources for all issues relating to aging.

learn.union-psce.edu/aging: A pastoral resource for older adults and their families, including an annotated bibliography.

www.ajas.org: A unique forum that promotes and supports elder services in the context of Jewish values through education, professional development, advocacy, and community relationships.

2

The Congregation as a Caring Community: Providing Support for Caregivers

Do not separate yourself from the community.
Pirkei Avot 2:4

In a place where no one acts as a human being, strive to be a human being.
Pirkei Avot 2:6

This chapter will address the following needs:

• Building a caring community for caregivers, their families, and those for whom care is being provided
• Honoring the *shomeir* (caregiver) and the mitzvah of caregiving through Jewish prayers and blessings

Contemporary society has created a new life stage: the caregiver. Yes, we have always had people who have been involved in this role. However, given the realities of the longevity revolution, the miracles of medical technology, and the challenges inherent in many of our health care systems, the caregiving role has taken on new importance. To be a caregiver is perhaps one of the greatest expressions of love. It is also a life stage for which few "volunteer." Rather, this role is entered into gradually or, for some, suddenly, when a phone call comes informing us that our life has changed. For years, many have referred to the so-called sandwich generation. Now, given the realities of life and longevity, mobility and family dynamics, it is no longer unusual for caregivers to be in what we call the "club sandwich," a multigenerational caregiving role that further taxes the caregiver and the caregiver's family. Many are now, for years, caught between the demands of work, family, personal dreams, and caring for a loved one.

For many, becoming a caregiver can be a daunting proposition. Those who are confronting the task for the first time are suddenly faced with questions that perhaps they had never considered. Financial and physical care issues may seem overwhelming. However, they may soon come to realize that there is something positive and sacred to caring for a loved one. A spiritual metamorphosis occurs wherein the caregiver is confronted with a wholly new spiritual dimension.

The ever-changing world in which we live, therefore, presents caregivers and congregations alike with the following challenge: how can congregations respond to the increasing need for caregivers to find support from within their synagogues? Congregations, for their part, must respond by creating programs that give support to these caregivers. In this way, the sanctity of relationships between and among families within the congregation is strengthened.

Judaism has always supported the notion that a connection exists between caregiving and maintaining loving, personal relationships. The quotations from *Pirkei Avot* at the beginning of the chapter remind us that we are all part of a living, organic spiritual community in which we are in potential relationship each with the other. We are, the tradition reminds us, responsible for each other's well-being, and that includes responsibility for providing love and support when a caregiver is called into action. Moreover, our Jewish values regarding caregiving are explicitly commanded in the Torah mandate to "honor and respect" our parents. In fact, this injunction is included in the daily prayer book, in which we are reminded that honoring our parents is an action whose reward is without measure. There is even a commentary on Proverbs 3:9 that parallels honoring parents with honoring God and says that "we honor through our financial resources as well as material and psychological resources."[1]

In developing a model for creating positive, nurturing caregiving relationships, congregations must not ignore the role of spirituality and God. "The link between how we take care of our loved ones and our relationship with God is an often neglected and much denied subtlety of the caregiving experience."[2] Because caregiving can place an overwhelming amount of stress on our emotional, physical, financial, and spiritual health, it is incumbent on congregations to find ways to help support and care for the caregiver.

One way to do this is through honoring the caregivers (*shomrim*) within our congregations. A caregiver can be someone other than a close friend or a family member of an older person; a caregiver may also be a congregation member, a professional assistant, a nurse, or any person who regularly reaches out to one in need. In each of these relationships there is something sacred that is developed between the caregiver and the one being cared for. It is important for congregations to recognize all the different caregivers in a person's life, to show them gratitude, and to strengthen their resolve to continue their efforts in a compassionate, loving manner.

Caregiving can be full of joy, wonder, and fulfillment. The synagogue is the setting to nurture those sentiments. We should celebrate the work of the caregiver! Special services that include prayers and blessings acknowledging their work help give caregivers emotional support. Moreover, programs that deal with the hands-on challenges of caregiving, coupled with a unique Jewish perspective to such challenges, help create a culture of support within congregations.

---

1. Richard F. Address and Hara E. Person, eds., *That You May Live Long: Caring for Our Aging Parents, Caring for Ourselves* (New York: UAHC Press, 2003), p. 3.
2. Ibid.

Establishing a Caregiver Program in Your Congregation

Gauge a country's prosperity by its treatment of the aged.
Rabbi Nachman of Bratzlav

Our community has the opportunity to choose to accept the responsibility of building a caring community that stretches a safety net of resources beneath its adult caregivers and their aging family members.[3] As synagogues are responding to the needs of older adults with programming for those who are healthy, additional programs and services are also needed for frail older adults and their caregivers. What follows is a sample assessment tool for caregivers that may help start a dialogue within your congregation on "caring for the caregiver."

Caregiver Survey

Are you an adult caregiver? Yes _____ No _____

Please check your age category.

_____ 25–35

_____ 35–45

_____ 45–55

_____ 55–65

_____ Over 65

Are you a long-distance adult caregiver (greater than 35 miles away)? Yes _____ No _____

Are you interested in attending a caregiver support meeting? Yes _____ No _____

Would you like to be contacted about a caregiver support program? Yes _____ No _____

Are you familiar with the social service networks in your local area? Yes _____ No _____
Please describe:

Do you want your clergy to be involved in your caregiving decisions? Yes _____ No _____
Please describe how the clergy can assist you in this area:

Does your congregation have a caring community committee? Yes _____ No _____

Which of the following issues are your major concerns? Check all that apply:

---

3. Judith Stevens-Long, *Adult Life-Developmental Processes* (Los Angeles: Mayfield, 1979).

____ Finding people who can help me or my loved one, whether local or long distance

____ Coping with a relative's declining mental and/or physical capabilities

____ Understanding the aging process from a Jewish perspective

____ Finances, Medicare, and health insurance information

____ Respite-care services/medical day-care services

____ Alternate living arrangements and options

____ How to access the social service network

____ Health advocate and consumer information

____ How to evaluate nursing homes

____ Making decisions

____ Dealing with guilt

____ Other (please identify): _____

If you care to, please describe the type of care you are currently giving (e.g., the kinds of tasks you perform, the number of hours a day you spend giving such care, the legal and/or financial burdens).

Name and address (optional): _____

_____

_____

Telephone and e-mail: _____

Caring Community Guidelines

The task of establishing a caring community and developing relevant and worthwhile programs can seem overwhelming without proper guidance and instruction. We strongly recommend that any congregation establishing a caring community first contact the URJ Press (**www.urjpress.com**) to purchase *Becoming a Kehillat Chesed: Creating and Sustaining a Caring Congregation*, by Harriet Rosen (New York: URJ Press, 2005). This publication includes a number of steps to follow in establishing a caring community. The congregational leadership may want to read the following additional guidelines[4] before beginning the process:

---

4. Adapted from a document created by Temple David, Monroeville, Pennsylvania.

1. **Identify members in your congregation who are caring for aging family members, either locally or from a distance.**
   a. Form a task force or committee to ascertain the major needs and concerns of your caregivers. Distribute needs assessment surveys to identify primary issues: long-distance caregiving, loss of parent's mental and/or physical abilities, moving in with one of the children, and other issues.
   b. Provide information on URJ publications and materials relating to issues on aging. Share with these families that they are not alone and that resource persons and materials are now available from their congregations and the URJ.
   c. Organize a task force to identify local and long-distance resources for caregiving. Congregations throughout the country are engaging in such a process within their local communities as well as providing information and support for the long-distance caregiver.
   d. Establish a congregational-based support network. Identify congregational leaders who can serve as resource persons to assist caregivers. Identify and train caregiver resource persons to be available at mutually convenient times to respond to the questions and needs of caregivers. Assistance in developing this type of training is available through the URJ Department of Jewish Family Concerns.
   e. Work with URJ national and local/regional professionals to initiate the process of identifying resources. In some smaller communities, local resources may be quite limited; it may be necessary to look to regional resources and the secular community. Establish links between Reform congregations, Jewish Federation agencies, other Jewish organization and congregations, and the secular community.
   f. Document local and long-distance caregiver resources. Make sure that this information is readily available.
   g. Publicize efforts of your congregational task force through synagogue newsletters, community newspapers, Shabbat services, brunches and meetings, e-mails, and bulletin boards.
   h. Plan periodic evening/half-day/weekend workshops and conferences to address the needs of caregivers. Offer regular caregiver support groups or special meetings that might feature a speaker or special discussion topic. A congregational leader or older-adult staff person can lead the group. Featured speakers might include physicians, nurses, attorneys, dentists, financial planners, recreation specialists, and other professionals.
   i. Commit yourself and your congregation to the establishment and maintenance of older adult programming and family-centered caregiver support programs.

2. **Identify older persons in your congregation who want to maintain their independence while they are aging in place.**
   a. Form a task force or committee to ascertain the major needs and concerns of your older congregants. Involve your older adults in collecting this information. Find out where the families of these older adults live or can be reached in the event of an emergency.
   b. Be prepared to specifically address the concerns identified by seniors regarding present and/or future needs for caregiver services and supportive services.
   c. Begin to locate and document resources within your community in the event of an illness, accident, or family crisis.
   d. Provide information on URJ publications and materials relating to issues on aging. Share with seniors that resource persons and materials are available from their congregations and from the URJ.

e. Encourage your older adult members to plan ahead while they are well by setting up advance directives, durable powers of attorney, and so on.

f. Organize a synagogue committee to identify local and regional resources for caregiving. (This can be done as an intergenerational or family track project.) Make the information easily and readily available to older adults. A good place to begin is with Jewish Federation agencies if they exist in your area.

g. Identify and train congregational leaders who can serve as resource persons to provide telephone contacts, hospital visitation, and other caregiving services for your older congregants. Name senior support resource persons who can respond to the concerns and questions of seniors. Provide specific times that these persons can be contacted by phone or in person.

h. Encourage older adults and seniors to contact the synagogue when they are in need of caregiver services. A great many older adults do not wish to be a burden and might not want to indicate that they need help. As people become older, they will eventually need some types of supportive services, even if it is only a ride to the synagogue to attend services. If seniors really believe that the congregation is committed to helping out, they will be more likely to ask for help when other needs arise.

i. Publicize the efforts of your older adult task force or committee through your synagogue newsletters, community newspapers, Shabbat services, brunches and meetings, bulletin boards, and e-mails. Published materials should have large, clear, and high-contrast printing, so as to be usable by older adults.

j. Plan half-day programs with lunch or refreshments to respond to the needs of your older members on a regular and continuing basis. In addition to providing a social opportunity for older adults, this type of event should be meaningful. Congregational leaders should also be present. Be prepared to really listen to what people are saying and act on their suggestions.

k. Plan special Shabbat services and other events that will specifically speak to issues and needs of older congregants. Look to creating new types of worship services that commemorate life-cycle events for older adults, such as retiring, moving from the family home, recovering from illness, and so on. Ask older persons to take active roles in planning these events.

l. Commit yourself and your congregation to the establishment and continuation of older adult programming, caregiving, and supportive services.

3. **Bring older adults and caregivers together.**

a. If your congregation's caregiver or older adult populations are large enough and the needs are identified, you may want to combine caregivers and seniors on a task force or committee together. (Recognize, however, that many caregivers are already themselves older adults.)

b. If your congregation's caregiver or older adult populations are not adequate for major programs, think about individual approaches to caring for persons within your congregation who need caregiver services. Select two or three interested persons who can provide telephone reassurance or who will begin to identify your community's resources. Make the information available in your library. Update materials at least annually.

c. Tap into the skills of older adult members in your congregation. A great many older adults in our congregations are active, healthy, and vital. Even frail older adults can participate in caring programs, providing telephone reassurance for each other.

d. Try to involve young children, adolescents, and young adults in developing and participating in caregiver programs. This provides excellent opportunities for intergenerational relationships, emotional support, and learning experiences for all.

Additional Programming Suggestions

Throughout this book, you will learn of many different programming ideas that you may wish to implement at your congregation. Below are some programming ideas that give support to caregivers and their families.

Provide Support Groups for Caregivers, Local and Long Distance

Begin to develop support groups and programs for members who are charged with caregiving. Use the resources of your caring community committee to help in transportation, respite care, networking, or resources for long-distance caregiving.

Provide Adult Day Care, Respite Care, Nutrition, Congregant Meals

Explore ways in which your congregation can be used as an adult day-care facility or nutrition center to help educate caregivers while at the same time easing the burden that some caregivers may feel. Look into developing respite-care programs for families, and use such programs to also help train caregivers and give them support.

Develop a "Care for the Caregiver" Program

Develop a one-day program that focuses on caregiving identity issues, feelings of guilt and fear, a desire to seek help, and the need to take care of one's own life in the face of caregiving demands. Teach caregivers to access and explore spirituality as a resource.[5]

Use an "Ombudsperson"

An "ombudsperson" is someone who will act as a contact and resource within the congregation, assisting the clergy by being a congregation-based resource for member families, providing immediate resources and referrals about caregiving issues. This person can work one-on-one with members to help them with legal, financial, and health-related issues. The ombudsperson can also develop seminars that assist caregivers and their loved ones in navigating the maze that often confronts them as they deal with things such as health insurance forms, benefit eligibility, and access to local resources.

Develop a "Person-to-Person" Referral Program

Someone who has previously dealt with a situation that a caregiver is suddenly confronted with can be a tremendous source for help and support in times of crisis or a sudden illness. Below is an example of a form that was created to implement a referral program.

---

5. Fern Ziegler and Heidi Waldmann developed such a program and presented it at Old York Road Temple–Beth Am of Abington, Pennsylvania. Please contact Temple Beth Am (215-886-8000, **www.oyrtbetham.org**) for more information.

Sample Resource Assessment Survey[6]

Our caring community wants to create a *Panim L'Panim* (Face to Face) network. The goal is to link those beginning a life experience with someone who has already lived it. Someone who has been there can bring comfort and support when it is most needed.

All information will remain confidential. Only the clergy and the network chair will see this information. **No information will be released without your prior permission.** All volunteers must participate in the temple's training program,[7] and problems beyond the volunteers' scope will be referred to the clergy or a professional resource.

Please fill out this form and return it in the enclosed envelope by (date). Thank you for your willingness to share your life experiences with others.

Please check any topics with which you have life experience and about which you are willing to talk to someone else.

Death of

_____ Parent   Date _____   Cause _____

_____ Spouse   Date _____   Cause _____

_____ Child   Date _____   Cause _____

_____ Sibling   Date _____   Cause _____

_____ Close friend Date _____   Cause _____

Long-term illness/disability of

_____ Parent   Date _____   Cause _____

_____ Spouse   Date _____   Cause _____

_____ Child   Date _____   Cause _____

_____ Sibling   Date _____   Cause _____

_____ Close friend Date _____   Cause _____

Your long-term illness

Illness _____   Dates _____

Dealing with/dealt with (either yourself or someone else)

_____ Cancer   Yourself _____   Someone else _____

(type of cancer: _____)

_____ Heart disease Yourself _____   Someone else _____

_____ Alcoholism   Yourself _____   Someone else _____

---

6. Adapted from Rosen, *Becoming a Kehillat Chesed*, p. 9.
7. For guidelines for creating a training program for volunteers, see Rosen, *Becoming a Kehillat Chesed*.

___ Stroke	Yourself ___	Someone else ___
___ Drug addiction	Yourself ___	Someone else ___
___ Parkinson's disease	Yourself ___	Someone else ___
___ Mental illness	Yourself ___	Someone else ___
___ Alzheimer's/dementia	Yourself ___	Someone else ___
___ HIV	Yourself ___	Someone else ___

What would you be willing to do?

___ Participate in a healing service or a service honoring caregivers

___ Lead a healing service or a service honoring caregivers

___ Visit a homebound person

___ Visit someone giving care to a person with a similar illness or disability

___ Take someone to a support group

___ Take someone to a treatment facility

___ Provide general support and/or consultation

What is/was your profession? Do you have any training in the fields checked above? Please

describe: _____

Are you willing to participate in Temple Shalom's training program for all volunteers in this

program? ___ Have you ever had this kind of training? ___ If yes, where and when?

_____

What format would best enable you to attend?

___ One day (Sunday)　　　___ Two or three midweek evenings

___ Two or three Sunday mornings

Thank you for your help,
Chair's name and clergy/Jewish professional's name

Develop a Training/Preparation Seminar for Caregivers

A one-week intensive training seminar that touches upon many issues caregivers face will help caregivers understand and cope with caring for their loved ones. Both caregivers and the ones who they are caring for would benefit from learning about the numerous mental, physical, and even financial considerations that go into taking care of a loved one. Here is an example of one such seminar:

Honor Your Father and Mother: A Time to Prepare[8]

1. Honoring Our Mothers and Fathers
    a. Overview of seminar series
    b. Discussion on how Judaism views parent-child relationships, responsibilities, and the fifth commandment
    c. A panel of synagogue members who will share their personal experiences, including dying parent living with adult child, parents who have not planned financially or legally, parents who are in denial, long-distance parent care, long-term illness, and navigating the medical system

2. Caring for the Caregiver
    (A panel discussion including a home health care specialist, a geriatric psychiatrist, and a health care manager)
    a. Exploration of caregiving and the impact that caring for a loved one has on one's own family and one's own psyche
    b. Learning coping strategies to minimize the burdens, and where to turn for spiritual, psychological, and financial support
    c. Developing resources for a parent far away
    d. Home care relief, and finding the right care manager

3. Financial and Legal Issues Associated with Caregiving
    (A panel discussion including an elder law attorney, a certified financial planner, and an insurance broker specializing in long-term care insurance)
    a. Proper planning to avoid a health or financial crisis
    b. Conservatorships: when there is no preplanning
    c. Long-term insurance coverage

4. Exploring Available Living Options
    (A panel discussion including a home health care specialist, a clinical coordinator/family consultant specializing in mental illnesses and/or Alzheimer's disease, and an elder law attorney)
    a. In-home, independent versus nursing home options
    b. Assisted-living care versus acute hospital care
    c. The role of the geriatric care manager
    d. Geriatric care management for out-of-town parents
    e. Adjustment to the "new home"
    f. Medicare benefits (even with sufficient assets)

5. Making Sacred Decisions at the End of Life
    (A panel discussion including a rabbi, a physician specializing in oncology, an elder law attorney, and a mortuary director)
    a. Legal end-of-life issues
    b. The Jewish approach to ethical decision making at the end of life
    c. Traditional Jewish views on active and passive euthanasia, assisted death, and pain management
    d. Current legislation on bioethics and related issues of competency
    e. Funeral arrangements: where to begin, preplanning

---

8. Partially adapted from a program entitled "Honor Your Father and Mother: A Six Session Series," hosted by Temple Israel of Hollywood, California. Each session was scheduled for two hours.

6. The Synagogue as Caregiver: A Healing Service
   a. Healing service led by a rabbi and cantor
   b. Opportunities for outreach to "adult children" and aging members of the synagogue
   c. Lunch with an open forum for the sharing of ideas

Prayers and Blessings: Creating a Shabbat Honoring *Shomrim*, the Caregivers in Your Congregation

Prayer works. Whether we are mourning, celebrating, worrying, or feeling contented, prayer has that magical way of bringing us closer to our feelings and our sense of wonderment.

In Judaism, there are prayers for almost every act one performs during the waking day. From the time we get up in the morning until we finally go to sleep, our Jewish tradition provides us with literally hundreds of prayers and blessings to concretize the moment. No act, it seems, is too mundane that it is not deserving of being made sacred on some level. Even when we awake in the morning, for example, our prayer book provides us with a number of prayers to recite as we go through our morning activities.

Rabbi Abraham Joshua Heschel once wrote:

> Holiness in space, in nature, was known in other religions. New in the teaching of Judaism was that the idea of holiness was gradually shifted from space to time, from the realm of nature to the realm of history, from *things* to *events*. . . . There were no naturally sacred plants or animals any more. To be sacred, a thing had to be consecrated by a conscious act of man. The quality of holiness is not in the grain of matter. It is a preciousness bestowed upon things by an act of consecration and persisting in relation to God.[9]

Acts of love are perhaps the most beautiful moments in our lives when we can bring a sense of the holy into the act. In the very nature of what they do, caregivers spend hours each day nurturing and providing love to someone else. Heeding Rabbi Heschel's words, therefore, it is worthwhile to explore creating prayers and blessings for the many acts of love that caregivers perform.

For example, in piloting programs for the Sacred Aging project, several congregations developed special services that honored caregivers. These *shomrim* (from the Hebrew root *shin-mem-reish,* which has the connotation of "taking care") often bear the responsibility of caregiving alone. Too often, our congregations do not take the opportunity to recognize and thank our members who devote large amounts of time and money to fulfilling the mitzvah of caregiving. What we ask is for our congregations to create an annual event at which they honor this growing population of caregivers. In honoring them, we honor what is best in us and model, for future generations, what proper Jewish value-based behavior is all about. Such pilot sites as Temple Sholom in Chicago, Illinois, and Temple Israel in West Palm Beach, Florida, helped create the environment that we hope will become a regular part of your congregational year. To help sustain these endeavors, we include pieces of liturgy that can be added to portions of a regular service, such as at the end of a *Mi Shebeirach*

---

9. Abraham Joshua Heschel, *The Sabbath* (New York: Farrar, Straus and Giroux, 1951), p. 79.

prayer. Alternatively, an entire service can be created that celebrates the joys of caregiving, provides support for caregivers, and honors them for their tireless efforts.

Honoring the caregiver is meant to be inspirational and spiritual. Yet, on a practical level, it is also supposed to bring both the *shomeir* and the aged a renewed sense of resolve and determination.

We hope that you will find these prayers and blessings both meaningful and useful in honoring the *shomrim* among the members of your congregation.

Prayers for Healing or During an Illness

1. This prayer could be read before reading or singing the *Mi Chamochah*:

Encountering the Desert[10]

There are three regions in each of our souls:
There is Egypt,
There is the Desert,
And there is the Promised Land.

Many of us have glimpsed our Egypt
Or perhaps some are still there,
Wearing the chains,
Bearing the burdens of fear, insecurity,
Doubt and weakness,
Mustering the strength to clamber up.

Still fewer of us have glimpsed the Promised Land,
Our destiny,
Fulfillment of dreams,
Our fruitfulness, our blossoming,
Our purpose.

We talk of Egypt often.
Every holiday, every prayer service
Mentions we once were slaves,
Recalls our hardship under Pharaoh.

We talk of the Promised Land often.
Every holiday, every prayer service
Longs for Israel,
For the Voice to come forth from Zion.
We turn to the east,
Reminisce Jerusalem.

---

10. By Rabbi Zoe Klein, in "Healing Service and Honoring Caregivers in Our Community," Temple Sholom, Chicago, IL, 2004.

But rarely do we talk of, or pray about, the Desert.
Yet that is the region in which most of us are,
Pushing forward in the wilderness,
Dragging our footsteps across that forty-year stretch
Of pristine, barren moonscape.

It is there we encounter truth.
It is there we encounter miracle.

We are nomads still,
At the shore of some sparkling oasis,
And we sing our nomad song . . .

בָּרוּךְ אַתָּה יְיָ, הַפּוֹרֵשׂ סֻכַּת שָׁלוֹם עָלֵינוּ.

Baruch atah Adonai, haporeis sukat shalom aleinu.

Blessed are You, *Adonai*, whose shelter of peace is spread over us.

2. This prayer could be read out loud at a service or used as a silent meditation:

Surround Me with Stillness[11]

Surround me with stillness,
Tiny ripples spreading across the pond,
Touched by one finger of Your hand,
Calmed by the warmth of Your palm.

Croon the wordless melody
That fills my being with peace.

Under the spreading tree of Your affection,
I will sit and meditate
On the goodness You have brought,
Counting the happy moments like glistening beads
Strung to adorn my days.

Light the shadowed corners with gentle glow,
To fill my being with peace.

Drape about me the dappled sunlight of Your teachings,
Opening my eyes to the search,
Clearing my heart of small distractions
That I might find the answers within myself.

---

11. By Debbie Perlman (*z"l*) and adapted from "Healing Service and Honoring Caregivers in Our Community."

Blow the breeze of compassion upon my brow,
Breathing the sigh of peace.

Let me rest by the water,
Probing gently for the sense of what I see,
Releasing my hurts to restore my spirit,
Feeling You guide me toward a distant shore.

3. This reading could also be used as a way to honor caregivers, since it deals with both the theme of healing and the theme of caring for others:

Two Sets of Tablets[12]

In the Talmud we are taught that the Ark held both the shattered fragments of the first set of tablets and the whole, unbroken second set. While we never lose our brokenness, we can become whole again—we can embrace our shattered hearts. We can become more compassionate, caring, and forgiving because we feel our brokenness when we share the pain of others. In our souls we carry both sets of tablets.

4. Reading responsively allows the congregation to feel like they are a part of the service. This reading implores God to help us heal:

Source of Life: Heal Us![13]

Leader: When Miriam was sick, her brother Moses prayed: "O God, heal her please!" We pray for those who are now ill. Source of Life, we pray.

Congregation: Source of Life, heal us!

Leader: We pray for those who are affected by illness, anguish, and pain.

Congregation: Source of Life, heal us.

Leader: Grant courage to those whose bodies, holy proof of Your creative goodness, are violated by illness and pain.

Congregation: Source of Life, encourage us.

Leader: Grant strength and compassion to families and friends who give their loving care and support, and help them to overcome despair.

Congregation: Source of Life, strengthen us.

Leader: Grant wisdom to those who probe the deepest complexities of Your world as they labor in the search for treatment and cures.

---

12. By Rabbi Sheldon Zimmerman, from "Healing Service and Honoring Caregivers in Our Community."
13. Adapted from Perlman, "Healing Service and Honoring Caregivers in Our Community."

Congregation: Source of Life, inspire us.

Leader: Grant clarity of vision and strength of purpose to the leaders of our institutions and our government. May they be moved to act with justice and compassion and find the courage to overcome fear and hatred.

Congregation: Source of Life, guide us.

Leader: Grant insight to us, that we may understand that whenever death comes, we must accept it—but that before it comes, we must resist it, by making our life worthy as long as it is lived.

Congregation: Source of Life, bless and heal us all. Amen.

5. Although this prayer confronts the physical illness of a loved one, it can also be used to ask God for mental or spiritual restoration for the caregiver:

When Fears Multiply[14]

When fears multiply
And danger threatens;
When sickness comes,
And death confronts us;

It is God's blessing of shalom
That sustains us
And upholds us,

Lightening our burden,
Dispelling our worry,
Restoring our strength,
Renewing our hope,

Reviving us.

Honoring Caregivers

1. This blessing could be said at the end of a service to bestow the special Priestly Benediction upon a caregiver or group of caregivers:

בִּרְכַּת קְהִילָה/Birkat K'hilla[15]

יְבָרֶכְךָ יְיָ וְיִשְׁמְרֶךָ

Y'varech'cha Adonai v'yishm'recha.

---

14. From "Renewing Life/Finding Wholeness," Temple Israel, Tulsa, Oklahoma.
15. Adapted from Perlman, "Healing Service and Honoring Caregivers in Our Community."

You sustain and nourish us with the sacred wisdom and traditions of our people,
teaching Torah to us and to our children.
May God bless you and keep you.

יָאֵר יְיָ פָּנָיו אֵלֶיךָ וִיחֻנֶּךָּ.

Ya-eir Adonai panav eilecha vichunecha.
You work alongside us to bring the light of justice and compassion
to God's broken world.
May God's face shine upon you, and may God always be gracious to you.

יִשָּׂא יְיָ פָּנָיו אֵלֶיךָ וְיָשֵׂם לְךָ שָׁלוֹם.

Yisa Adonai panav eilecha v'yaseim l'cha shalom.
You bear witness to our lives and accompany us on our journey;
You help us elevate our consciousness and search in every hour
for God's presence in our lives.

For the care you give to our community,
may God lift your hearts and grant you
wholeness, fulfillment, and peace.

2. This prayer reflects the joy and apprehension that we all sometimes feel when we reach
out to help others:

We Serve God with Joy

Leader: There is much that burdens us, weighs us down.

Congregation: It is time to put down our burdens.

Leader: Let us name our fears and guilt, our longings and our pain.

Congregation: Perhaps then we can set it all aside, at least for a moment, and be fully
present in this time with one another.

Leader: Let us pray, trusting in the power of the Eternal One.

Congregation: O Spirit of compassion and care, there are so many times when I feel
inadequate to the job of caring, so overwhelmed with the enormity of the tasks
involved. It is in those moments that I feel I have been abandoned, forgotten, tested
in some ultimate way, not equal to the reality that stares me in the face.

Leader: There are other times when I am sure that I am being taken for granted, unap-
preciated, perhaps not even noticed.

Congregation: I have moments when I know that I am failing to do enough and am
incapable of doing anything right.

Leader: As we turn toward Shabbat, I pray that my mind be less troubled. My thoughts are more peaceful and tranquil, and my courage grows, as I reflect on these words.

Congregation: I will hope continually, and will praise You more and more. Yes, there is hope in me, for it may be that tomorrow I shall put forth buds again, and clothe myself in fruit.

בָּרוּךְ אַתָּה יְיָ, שׁוֹמֵעַ תְּפִלָּה.

Baruch atah Adonai, shomei-a t'filah!

Blessed are You, O God, who hearkens to prayer!

3. This meditative piece acknowledges the emotional difficulties that often confront a caregiver:

A Meditation for Caregivers[16]

All of us at some time in our lives have been caregivers—for parents, children, spouses, friends, and each other. Go inside yourself for a moment and relive what it was like to give care to others.

Think of those for whom you have taken the responsibility to tend to their needs at a time when they could not.

Now go deeper into yourself and recall the times that others cared for you. Imagine your caregivers in your heart and your mind.

Go even deeper and imagine the love and dedication they felt for you.

Take a moment. See it. Feel it. Hear the sounds of their voices.

As we find comfort in the shelter of God, we can find comfort on earth through the loving-kindness of others.

4. This blessing includes the entire community in asking for courage on behalf of our caregivers:

A Prayer for Those Who Help[17]

May the One who blessed our ancestors be present to those who provide help for the ill and troubled among us. May they be filled with fortitude and courage, endowed with sympathy and compassion, as they give strength to those at their side. May they fight against despair, and continue to find within themselves the will to reach out to those in need. And in their love of others, may they know the blessing of community, and the blessing of renewed faith. Amen.

---

16. From "A Caregiver's Shabbat," ed. Stan Levin, Temple Emanuel, Kensington, MD, 2002.
17. From "Renewing Life/Finding Wholeness."

5. This reading reminds us how sacred and holy the mitzvot of caring for another person can be:

To Face Sacred Moments[18]

Rabbi Abraham Heschel said, "The higher goal of spiritual living is not to amass a wealth of information, but to face sacred moments." When God and Moses met on Mt. Sinai, the focus was on what it was that human beings needed in the way of boundaries in order that life could be lived in a purposeful, meaningful way. Thus we learn: "Honor your mother and father so that you may live a long time in the land that I, Adonai your God, am giving to you."

It has been known from the beginning of time that when we all take care of those within our own family who need our care, we are showing them respect and honor. Even more, we are opening ourselves, as Rabbi Heschel reminds us, to the experience of sacred moments. When someone in our family is weak, disabled, fragile, vulnerable, sick, aging, or dying, the presence of God is often mediated through the family's care, and conversely, in giving care. May you be blessed, just as you are a blessing!

On Life's Journeys

1. This traditional prayer focuses on the things that we wish for as we continue our journey through life:

The Traveler's Prayer / תְּפִלַת הַדֶרֶךְ

Adonai shall guard your coming and your going from this time forth and forever.

Adonai, the whole world is full of Your glory. Wherever I go, You are near to me. If I take up the wings of the morning and dwell on the ocean's farthest shore, even there Your hand will lead me; Your right hand will hold me.

You have always been a light to my path. Now that I begin another journey, I turn to You in confidence and trust. Protect me from the perils of the way. May I go forth in health and safely reach my destination. May this journey not be in vain; let its purpose be fulfilled; let me return in contentment to my dear ones. Then shall I know Your blessing in all my travels. *Amen.*

2. Both caregivers and those who are being cared for can find inspiration in this meditation, which harkens us to recall the wonders and beauties of life:

The Evening's Twilight[19]

Let me do my work each day;
And if dark hours of despair overcome me,

---

18. From "A Caregiver's Shabbat."
19. Created by Hevreh of Southern Berkshire, Great Barrington, Massachusetts.

May I not forget the strength that comforted me in times past.

May I still remember the bright hours that found me walking over the silent hills of my childhood,
Or dreaming on the margin of the quiet river, when light glowed within me. . . .

Lift my eyes from the earth, and let me not forget the uses of the stars.
Let me not follow the clamor of the world, but walk calmly in my path.

And should I not reach sight of the castle of my dreams, teach me still to be thankful for life and for time's golden memories that are good and sweet.

And may evening's twilight find me gentle still.

3. This prayer links the Torah to our life's journey, reminding us of the immeasurable value of our Jewish tradition during each phase of our lives:

In Each Age[20]

Leader: In each age we receive and transmit Torah.

   Congregation: At each moment we are addressed by the World.

In each age we are challenged by our ancient teaching.

   At each moment we stand face to face with truth.

In each age we add our wisdom to that which has gone before.

   At each moment the knowing heart is filled with wonder.

In each age the children of Torah become its builders, and seek to set the world firm on a foundation of Truth.

On Having to Be Helped

1. This prayer could be used at a service honoring both caregivers and their loved ones, as it asks for patience and understanding for those who are in need of help from their caregivers:

Needing Help[21]

God, I don't like to be helped. It makes me feel I am a burden and a nuisance. When I vent anger about my affliction, let me do it privately and with frustration only

---

20. By Rabbi Rami Shapiro.
21. From "Renewing Life/Finding Wholeness."

toward my circumstances, and not toward those who help me. When I must ask for assistance, let my words be gentle. Let me remember to say "please" with even my simplest request and "thank you" when even my smallest bidding is granted. Let me do all that I can for myself. But give me the wisdom to know the difference between self-reliance and foolhardiness. Amen.

2. This reading describes how those who are in need of help should allow their caregivers to give them the love and attention they need:

Give Me Your Hand[22]

Jewish tradition teaches that it is important to allow others to help us when we are sick. According to midrash, Rabbi Yochanan visited Rabbi Chanina during the latter's illness. When Rabbi Chanina complained about his suffering, Rabbi Yochanan suggested that he speak the same encouraging words to himself that he had spoken with such good effect to Rabbi Yochanan when he was ill. Rabbi Chanina replied, "When I was free of sufferings, I could help others; but now that I am myself a sufferer, I must help others to help me." The meaning of this story is obvious but bears repeating: we should know both how to give and how to take, and that in taking, often we are also giving.

The Gift of Life

1. We should constantly remind ourselves how wonderful it is to be alive and to appreciate those faculties that still bring us joy, as this responsive reading reminds us:

Giving Thanks for Life[23]

Leader: We must often revive the gladness of gratitude. And retain our lips to utter words of thanks.

Congregation: God's gifts often go unnoticed in our haste. And disappointments may blind us to our blessings.

Leader: We render thanks for Life itself, for sight, hearing, smell, taste, and touch.

Congregation: We give thanks for the beauty of nature and its gifts. And we pray that we may share as richly as we have received.

Leader: We stand in wonder before the birth of children, the miracle of their growth, their love and laughter.

Congregation: We are grateful for love and the opening of hearts, between husband and wife, and between parents and children. Amen.

---

22. From Perlman, "A Healing Service Honoring Caregivers."
23. From "A Caregiver's Shabbat."

2. This prayer can either be read out loud or used as a meditational piece. It is a nice prayer to use either as an introduction or a conclusion to a service honoring caregivers.

A Blessing on the Occasion of a Life Transition[24]

Eternal God, Source of all life.
Thank You for giving me life.
Thank You for guiding my way,
And for helping me reach this season and this place.
Help me adjust to the changes in my life.
Help me mourn the losses I have known.
Open my eyes to new possibilities and new opportunities
for continued growth, for new relationships in my new home.
Bless my new home and watch over me.
Help my new home become a place
of comfort, connections, and community,
May You be a constant Presence
And Source of comfort in my life.

Amen.

Creative Religious Writing

Creating blessings and prayers to honor a caregiver is yet another programming idea that congregations can use to provide support to caregivers. There is something magical and cathartic about putting one's emotions down on paper in a sacred context. Writing religious prayers does more than just serve as a vehicle for expressing basic feelings of thanks, relief, salvation, hope, desire, celebration, and fear. The process of expressing one's emotions in the form of prayer serves a higher, ethical function as well. Creating poetry in the form of religious blessings helps us to clarify, differentiate our feelings. It helps us to choose which road to travel, what decisions we should make, and what blessings we wish for ourselves and the ones we love.[25]

Rabbi Gerald M. Kane of Temple Beth-El in Las Cruces, New Mexico, developed a spiritual writing course focusing on the Book of Psalms as a catalyst for caregivers to create their own psalms. Here are a few examples of religious poetry that Rabbi Kane's congregants created. Each one of them can be used in a service honoring and giving support to caregivers.

1. This piece gives thanks for the wonderful moments of awe that we experience throughout our lives:

Source of All Good[26]

Oh, Source of All Good,
It is past time to thank you for all of your sweet gifts.

24. By Dr. Debra Smith of the Lester Senior Housing Community in Whippany, New Jersey.
25. Adapted from Lance J. Sussman, *Sharing Sacred Moments* (Binghamton, NY: Keshet Press, 1999), p. 144.
26. Anonymous.

You are a Generous Healer and Forgiver,
and You have helped me to learn and give honest introspection
and unconditional love.

I send You silent daily prayers of gratitude for my caring husband,
my best friend.
I thank you for our wonderful children, and grandchildren;
they are Your most beloved gift.
As we mindfully bond together and cherish each other,
my feelings assure me that my memory
will be a source of blessing to them.

For the joy of live music, art and exultant words,
it is to You I turn to praise.
For the blessing of starting each day anew, forgiven, it is You
I combine all of my thankful being.

For the promise of each day to come,
For every one of Your Generous Moments,
I return my breath to You with Love.

2. Caregiving can be a source of joy and celebration, as this poem relates:

All of Our Days[27]

The length of my days
has become a list
   of things
   of duties
   of chores

to be checked off each evening:
   phone his doctor
   take him to the dentist
   pay our bills
   weed the garden

I must add to the list:
   Glory in sunrise
   Notice yellow flowers
   Listen to birds
   Enjoy life

Enjoy LIFE

---

27. Anonymous.

When my time comes
to ascend to the next plane
I hope I won't be greeted
by an angel
checking off my name
from a list
on a clipboard.

Enjoy life.

3. This poem praises God for all of the tasks performed in a day's work:

Giving Praise and Gratitude[28]

God is my Shepherd, I shall not want.
God is the author and finisher of my faith;
God wakes me in the morning;
God keeps me by night;
God places a hedge of protection around those I love and care for.

God clears my mind of the day's clutter;
God keeps me focused squarely on the Almighty;
God is the Alpha and the Omega.

My Creator writes my name in the Book of Life;
God grants me life eternal because of my faith in the Almighty;
I will praise God all the days of my life.

Sitting again in the waiting room of a hospital. Waiting with a parent to see another doctor. Making idle conversation and flashing back on so many moments in life when situations were reversed. No matter how prepared for such moments you think you are, the reality of caregiving challenges much of what we take for granted, daring us to examine our priorities.[29]

By honoring the caregivers within our congregational communities, we affirm the holiness of their deeds. We combine their actions with sanctity, resulting in stronger relationships between family and friends.

May the holy deeds of all who are charged with the task of caring for another be blessed with joy, happiness, and *shalom*—peace.

---

28. By Randy M. Castellano of Las Cruces, New Mexico.
29. Richard F. Address, "Introduction: Celebrating the Art of Caregiving," in *That You May Live Long: Caring for Our Aging Parents, Caring for Ourselves*, ed. Richard F. Address and Hara E. Person (New York: UAHC Press, 2003), p. 2.

Additional Resources

Books

Alzheimer's Disease and Dementia

Barrick, Ann L., et al. *Bathing without a Battle: Creating a Better Bathing Experience for Person's with Alzheimer's Disease*. Chapel Hill: University of North Carolina Press, 2004.

Bell, Virginia, and David Troxel. *The Best Friends Book of Alzheimer's Activities*. Baltimore: Health Professionals Press, 2004.

Forrest, Deborah. *Symphony of Spirits: Encounters with the Spiritual Dimensions of Alzheimer's*. New York: St. Martin's Press, 2000.

Harper, M. A. *The Worst Day of My Life, So Far: My Mother, Alzheimer's and Me*. New York: Harvest, 2001.

Mace, Nancy L. *The 36-Hour Day: A Family Guide to Caring for Persons with Alzheimer Disease, Related Dementing Illnesses, and Memory Loss in Later Life*. New York: Warner Books, 2001.

Markut, Lynda A. *Dementia Caregivers Share Their Stories: A Support Group in a Book*. Nashville: Vanderbilt University Press, 2005.

McKim, Donald, ed. *God Never Forgets: Faith, Hope and Alzheimer's Disease*. Louisville, KY: Westminster John Knox Press, 1997.

Post, Stephen. *The Moral Challenge of Alzheimer's Disease*. Baltimore: Johns Hopkins University Press, 1995.

Caregiver Support

Bagnull, Marlene. *My Turn to Care: Encouragement for Caregivers of Aging Parents*. Nashville: Thomas Nelson Publishers, 1994.

Berman, Claire. *Caring for Yourself While Caring for Your Aging Parents: How to Help, How to Survive*. New York: Henry Holt and Company, 2001.

Cluff, L. E., and R. H. Binstock, eds. *The Lost Art of Caring: A Challenge to Health Professionals, Families, Communities, and Society*. Baltimore: Johns Hopkins University Press, 2001.

Fox, Carole B. *Community Care for an Aging Society*. New York: Springer, 2005.

Johnson, Richard P. *Caring for Aging Parents*. St. Louis: Concordia Publishing House, 1997.

Morgan, Richard L. *From Grim to Green Pastures: Meditations for the Sick and Their Caregivers*. Nashville: Upper Room Press, 1999.

Rhodes, Linda M. *Caregiving as Your Parents Age*. New York: New American Library, 2005.

Richards, Marty. *Eldercare: The Best Resources to Help You Help Your Aging Relatives*. Issaquah, WA: Resource Pathways, 1999.

Death, Grief, and Loss

Callahan, Maggie, and Patricia Kelley. *Final Gifts: Understanding the Special Awareness, Needs and Communications of the Dying*. New York: Poseidon Press, 1992.

Cohen, Cynthia B., et al. *Faithful Living, Faithful Dying: Anglican Reflections on End-of-Life Care*. Harrisburg, PA: Moorehouse Publishing, 2000.

Kelley, Patricia. *Companion to Grief: Finding Consolation When Someone You Love Has Died*. New York: Simon & Schuster, 1997.

Rich, Phil. *The Healing Journey Through Grief: Your Journal for Reflection and Recovery.* New York: John Wiley & Sons, 1999.

Jewish Spirituality

Address, Richard E. and Hara E. Person, eds. *That You May Live Long: Caring for Our Aging Parents, Caring for Ourselves.* New York: UAHC Press, 2003. The Teacher's Guide is available through the URJ Department of Jewish Family Concerns.

Person, Hara E., ed. *The Mitzvah of Healing.* New York: UAHC Press, 2003.

Resources

Loverde, Joy. *Complete Eldercare Planner: Where to Start, Which Questions to Ask, and How to Find Help.* New York: Crown, 2000.

Richards, Marty. *Eldercare: The Best Resources to Help You Help Your Aging Relatives.* Issaquah, WA: Resource Pathways, 1999.

Videos

At Death's Door: Facing the Terminal Illness of a Loved One. Brewster, MA: Paraclete Press, 1999.

Beyond Death's Door: Help for the Grieving Process After Someone You Loved Has Died. Brewster, MA: Paraclete Press, 1999.

On Our Own Terms: Moyers on Dying. Available through Films for the Humanities and Sciences; phone (800) 257-5126.

Services for the Long Distance Care-giver. Available from Caring from a Distance. **www.cfad.org**.

Web Sites

Alzheimer's Disease and Dementia

www.alzstore.com: Obtain information on products for home safety and care for the Alzheimer's patient.

www.alz.org: The Alzheimer's Association lists local chapters that provide education and support for patients and their families.

Caregiver Support

www.caregiving.org: The National Alliance for Caregiving is a nonprofit coalition that provides information and resources for family caregivers and professionals.

www.seniorcareweb.com: Comprehensive caregiving and general eldercare information.

www.caregiver.com: *Today's Caregiver* magazine specializes in caregiving issues.

www.gu.org: Generations United supports grandparents and other relatives raising children.

www.nfcacares.org: The National Family Caregivers Association empowers family caregivers to advocate more persuasively on behalf of their loved ones with health care professionals.

www.carethere.com: Caregiver marketplace of services, caregiver guides, and answers to medication questions.

www.caregiverzone.com: Nationwide caregiver database on elder care resources.

www.caremanager.org: The National Association of Professional Geriatric Care Managers gives links to fee-based geriatric care managers (helpful for long-distance caregivers).

www.aarp.org/ageline: The AARP's web page contains resources for research on a variety of issues pertaining to aging and caregiving.

www.ascp.com: The American Society of Consulting Pharmacists' "Seniors Care Pharmacy" offers resources on drugs and prescription interactions.

Governmental Agencies/Guides

www.eldercare.gov: For a guide to available governmental resources and information on location of governmental agencies on aging (including local services, support groups, and legal assistance). You can also telephone an information specialist to help identify local services: (800) 677-1116.

www.n4a.org: The National Association of Area Agencies on Aging assists the aging population as well as health care providers, raising awareness for both groups.

www.benefitscheckup.org: For information on the availability of various governmental and medical benefits.

www.aoa.gov/prof/aoaprog/caregiver: For a comprehensive government guide that gives suggestions for caregivers.

Jewish Spirituality

www.jewishhealing.org: National Jewish Healing Center, offering a variety of services and resources.

www.ncjh.org: The National Center for Jewish Healing helps communities meet the spiritual needs of Jews living with illness, loss, and significant life challenges.

www.HealingPsalm.com: For guidance on how to develop a program on writing religious poetry.

www.songwritingworks.org: Songwriting Works teaches caregivers and elders alike the power of creating Jewish songs and poetry.

Legal

www.caregiver.org: The Family Caregiver Alliance/National Center on Caregiving gives free information on health conditions, care strategies, and legal and financial issues in a fifty-state survey.

www.naela.org: The National Academy of Elder Law Attorneys gives referrals to attorneys who specialize in law relating to aging and caregiving.

www.law4elders.com: For various legal publications and resource guides.

www.myziva.net: To check up on any specific nursing home or assisted-living facility to see what kinds of citations or deficiency notices it has received.

www.myltc.com: Insurance Solutions for Long Term Care provides special long-term care insurance offers to URJ congregants.

www.abanet.org/aging: Free publications on law and aging are available from the Commission on Law and Aging of the American Bar Association.

www.ama-assn.org/ama/pub/category/10791.html and **www.thehartford.com /alzheimers/warning.html:** Two resources on determining older adults' ability to continue driving.

3

Creating New Rituals
for Our Extended Life Span

Religion is not a way of satisfying needs. It is an answer to the question: Who needs man?
It is an awareness of being needed, of man being a need of God.
It is a way of sanctifying the satisfaction of authentic needs.
The central commandment is in relation to the person.
But religion today has lost sight of the person.

Abraham Joshua Heschel,
The Insecurity of Freedom: Essays on Human Existence, p. 8.

This chapter will address the following needs:

• Sanctifying life, time, and relationships with new rituals
• Creating and reinterpreting rituals for moments of loss, transition, and personal growth
• Developing new rituals to address the realities of older adults and their relationships

Our Reform Jewish tradition has always been accepting of new rituals and blessings to commemorate certain events. As our Jewish needs change, so have our prayers, blessings, and modes of worship changed. Our ability to adapt to new circumstances is what gives our Reform tradition its meaning and spirituality. It is also, as Heschel reminds us, what allows religion to respond to the needs of its members. In doing so, it helps forge the sacred relationship that exists between humankind, God, and a moment.

When liturgy is combined with ritual, one is able to experience a spiritual realm that is separate from the mundane. An example of this is our *Havdalah* service, in which we praise God for giving us the ability to appreciate the holiness of the Sabbath and the ordinariness of the weekdays. This ceremony, combined with the ritual of smelling the spices, drinking the wine, and holding the candle, elevates our appreciation for the sanctity of a passing Shabbat.

The same effect can occur during life-cycle changes within our own lives. Any task involving caring for someone else can be elevated through prayer and ritual, so that something holy takes place when performing that task. This, in turn, can help the older adult emotionally cope with what he or she is about to do.

This chapter includes rituals that enable us to move more easily and more deliberately through the stages of late life. The development of ritual is gradual and comes about mostly through consensus arrived at by experimentation. Because ritual, by its very nature, is symbolic, it involves more art than science. Including in rituals all of the five senses elevates the sense of awareness and brings the participants closer to the experience.[1]

Many view transformation as one of the key elements in religious ritual. Ritual allows for the individual to transition from one phase of life to another, often liberating that individual. The longevity revolution is now providing fresh opportunities to aid in this process of personal and cultural transformation by creating new rituals that respond to lifestyles and life cycles more diverse than in previous generations. The aging population presents us with a unique opportunity to connect older congregants with their values, wisdom, and experience. Everyone benefits in this creative culture, including the younger generation that inevitably will witness those values as they become symbolized and acted out in the new liturgy.

New Jewish Rituals

The Department of Jewish Family Concerns sponsored a number of workshops at URJ congregations that brought together older adults for the purpose of a discussion on creating new rituals for new life stages. Participants were asked to reflect on the life stages and events that have taken place within their lives, and think if and how their congregation could respond with appropriate rituals.

Some of the results of these sessions are provided in this chapter. Not surprisingly, many of the rituals that were suggested already exist within the Jewish tradition. Other traditional prayers were reincorporated into new pieces of liturgy dealing with the aging process. By doing this, there is a feeling that what we are creating is still rooted in Jewish tradition. Furthermore, the newly created ritual becomes an expression of a new idea, steeped in the tradition of an ancient Jewish ethic.

Many of the rituals represent a dramatic shift and do not incorporate any other traditional Jewish prayer. Nevertheless, their value in reacting to modern changing family dynamics cannot be overstated. Technological and medical advances throughout the past century have left us with gaps in Jewish ritual practice. For example, medicine has allowed adults to experience longer life spans than what we thought was possible. But along with such medical technology come new challenges, such as having to face lifestyle changes when one spouse succumbs to dementia.

Furthermore, the spiritual revolution within our communities has forced us to reevaluate other life-cycle events that occur as we age. Our desire to become renewed with our tradition at an older age, for example, should be recognized in a significant way. The recent interest among congregants to place their lives in a spiritual context forces congregations to consider how to ritualize moments such as removing the wedding ring after the death of a spouse, or retiring from a profession.

Both clergy and laypeople created the rituals that appear in this chapter. A brief introduction precedes each ritual. Where applicable, we have noted when we have reintroduced a rit-

---

1. From an article by Rev. Thomas B. Robb, reprinted in *Aging and Spirituality: The First Decade*, ed. James Ellor, Susan McFadden, and Stephen Sapp (San Francisco: American Society on Aging, 1999), p. 58.

ual that already exists in our tradition. The introduction also includes an explanation of how the ritual can be used and suggestions regarding who is appropriate to perform the ritual.

These rituals reflect issues and needs that are both real and substantial. It is our hope that you will revise and adapt these rituals to bring greater meaning into your own life.

Creating Special Moments

Upon Becoming a Grandparent

This blessing can be said at a *b'rit* or baby-naming ceremony or at a regular service before the congregation. It can be read by one grandparent or, if there are more, all of the grand-parents together. It can also be revised so that it ritualizes the arrival of a great-grandchild.

A Blessing for a Grandchild[2]

We are thankful for the many joys with which our life has been blessed. Now this great goodness has come to us: a new life, a new child to love, the opening of a new chapter in the chronicle of our family's existence. May this child grow up in health and happiness, to become a blessing to family, friends, and neighbors.

May her/his dear parents find much joy in the years that lie before them. Grant, O God, that they rear their child with wisdom and understanding, teaching him/her the ways of righteousness, leading him/her to the study of Torah and the practice of love and kindness.

And may we, too, be granted the joy of seeing him/her develop all his/her facul-ties, and the gratification of helping him/her to fulfill the best that is in him/her. Then our humble prayer shall have found its answer; the days and years to come shall be for us times of peace and wondrous fulfillment.

בָּרוּךְ אַתָּה יְיָ, אֱלֹהֵינוּ מֶלֶךְ הָעוֹלָם, שֶׁהֶחֱיָנוּ וְקִיְּמָנוּ וְהִגִּיעָנוּ לַזְּמַן הַזֶּה.

Baruch atah Adonai, Eloheinu melech haolam,
shehecheyanu v'kiy'manu v'higianu laz'man hazeh.

We praise You, Eternal God, Sovereign of the universe, for giving us life,
for sustaining us, and for enabling us to reach this season. Amen.

Celebrating a Special Birthday

These prayers recognize a special turn in someone's life: reaching a milestone in one's age. In many congregations, there is a special Family Shabbat where the rabbi gives a blessing for those congregants celebrating milestones, such as significant birthdays or anniversaries. The following readings can be said at such a moment.

A Special Birthday Blessing[3]

Reader: Judaism gives us many occasions to change ordinary days into sacred days. Through ceremonies, we can make a bris, a wedding, or a holiday into a special expe-

---

2. Anonymous.
3. Adapted from "Readings and Rituals for the Joys, Challenges, and Transitions of Senior Adulthood," published by the Jewish Council for the Aging, in collaboration with Temple Rodef Shalom, Falls Church, Virginia.

rience, bringing to the present moment the awareness that we are part of history and the values that transcend time and space.

Our special times are important, and your birthday is a special time for us. The idea of a *Simchat Ha-Dorot*—a "Rejoicing of the Generations"—is a new one, a chance for us to celebrate the blessings you have brought to our lives.

It is not unusual that we choose to honor you for your long life. Judaism teaches a respect for our elders. The Rabbis believed that age and wisdom went hand in hand and that it was proper to stand when an elderly person entered the room and then take a place at their feet. Our elders grow in wisdom through their life experiences, and each of us could grow from listening to their advice.

Congregation:

בָּרוּךְ אַתָּה יְיָ, אֱלֹהֵינוּ מֶלֶךְ הָעוֹלָם, הַמְאַפְשֵׁר לִי לַחֲלוֹק
חַיַּי עִם רֵעַ אָהוּב וְאוֹהֵב.

Baruch atah Adonai, Eloheinu Melech haolam,
ham'afsheir li lachalok chayai im rei-ah ahuv v'oheiv.

Reader: We praise You, Eternal God, Sovereign of the universe: You enable us to share life with a beloved and loving friend.

Congregation: Amen.

This next prayer can be accompanied by ritual items that help enhance the spirituality of the experience. Upon reaching a milestone birthday, Selma Sage of Toronto used various traditional Jewish pieces. She wrote the following piece describing her experience:

I recently celebrated a special birthday in a most unique way. A party had been planned with a small gathering of loving family and friends, to mark my new status as a senior citizen.

Rabbi Daveen Litwin sensitively introduced the *Simchat Chochmah* ritual to the group. She explained certain symbols that I had chosen in their Jewish sense, and I went on to define these symbols' importance in my life.

We used water, a symbol of cleansing, clarity, and rebirth. Then we used an apple, the eternal symbol not only of woman and woman's power, but also of future sweetness. A lighted candle signified a renewal of my commitment with the covenant of Judaism. The candle represented, for me, the light and warmth I have shared over the years as a teacher. Just as I shed light through my teaching, I am also illuminated so others can see me. Therefore, I must model my life Jewishly for others.

We then took a lovely fragrant rose and passed it among my guests, and while they held the rose, they were asked to bless me with a special memory or a birthday wish. The wishes and blessings were so remarkable I cried at their beauty. My guests dabbed at tears.

These objects signified a Jewish rite of passage that has served to validate and reaffirm my status as a Jewish woman of age in my community.

We then read the *Simchat Chochmah* blessing:

Simchat Chochmah / The Blessing of Wisdom[4]

River of light and truth, You have sustained me these many years and brought me to this place in my life's journey. Let me look out with wisdom, from the high ground of my years and experiences, over the terrain of my life. Let me gaze out toward the past and the future with a heightened sense of Your presence as my Guide. Let me see that growth is not reserved for any one season, and that love and fulfillment are not the exclusive provinces of the young.

As today I celebrate my life's continued unfolding, I am awestruck by the wonder of my being. And so I pray that kindness and compassion may be on my lips, that strength and courage may be with me in my comings and my goings, and that I may continue to learn from and to teach those dear to me.

O God my Creator, as You are the first and the last, may my life ever be a song of praise to You.

בָּרוּךְ אַתָּה יְיָ, אֱלֹהֵינוּ מֶלֶךְ הָעוֹלָם, שֶׁנָּתַן מֵחָכְמָתוֹ לְבָשָׂר וָדָם.

Baruch atah Adonai, Eloheinu Melech haolam,
shenatan meichochmato l'vasar vadam.

We praise You, Eternal God, Sovereign of the universe: You give
of Your wisdom to flesh and blood.

Amen.

Celebrating a Wedding Anniversary

A special anniversary, such as a silver or golden anniversary, can be a moment of tremendous joy and celebration. This ritual can be recited by the honored couple, either in the congregation or at a special gathering of friends and family.

Blessing for a Special Wedding Anniversary[5]

"I am my beloved's, and my beloved is mine." God of all generations, we give thanks for the blessings that have graced our marriage, and we look back upon the day of our union with thankfulness. So may this joy be with us always: our way of life loving and good, as we help each other bear burdens and as we share our joys.

Give us, O God, a peaceful dwelling where contentment and love find a resting-place. May we maintain a home in which glows the light of faith, one which honors our membership in the House of Israel, our people.

O God, grant that we may grow old together in health, and live in gratitude for our marriage.

---

4. Adapted from *On the Doorposts of Your House: Prayers and Ceremonies for the Jewish Home,* ed. Chaim Stern (New York: CCAR Press, 1994), p. 152.
5. Adapted from *On the Doorposts of Your House,* p. 136.

בָּרוּךְ אַתָּה יְיָ, אֱלֹהֵינוּ מֶלֶךְ הָעוֹלָם, שֶׁהֶחֱיָנוּ וְקִיְּמָנוּ וְהִגִּיעָנוּ לַזְּמַן הַזֶּה.

Baruch atah Adonai, Eloheinu melech haolam,
shehecheyanu, v'kiy'manu, v'higianu laz'man hazeh.

We praise You, Eternal God, Sovereign of the universe,
for giving us life, for sustaining us, and for enabling us to reach this season.

Senior Cohabitation

An opportunity to create new rituals based on changing lifestyles is presented by the number of older adults who choose to be together without the benefit of a formal marriage ceremony. As we live longer, these circumstances may increase. The situation is familiar to many of us: the widow or widower or the divorced man or woman who meets someone special and the couple, for a wide variety of reasons, choose to be together but not be legally married. They come to their clergyperson and ask for a blessing that will sanctify their being together. There is no issue of children. There is an issue of intimacy as one ages, the security of a caring partner and the need to thank God that two people have found each other and to ask for peace and comfort in the years that may be granted.

These types of living arrangements are no longer unfamiliar to us. As a result, congregations should provide rituals that take into consideration the very human need for intimacy and relationships. Genesis 2:18 is correct when it reminds us that it is not good that we go through life alone. The extended life spans that are now emerging will allow for more of these types of situations. Shall we just ignore them? Or shall we see in many of these relationships unique opportunities to develop something sacred and special to the many people who choose to come to their faith community and have this new relationship blessed? This ceremony is not a marriage, and this fact must be part of the discussions that lead to the ceremony. However, it is a ritual of thanks that people have found each other and a hope that they may find peace and security in the years ahead. In the end, the openness to the development of such unions allows for the continuing evolution of faith communities to the new realities presented by the dynamic changes in life spans and lifestyles.[6]

We have included here two rituals that can be used to bless a union between two people who together have decided to share their lives with one another. These two prayers were created after much consideration was given to the Jewish marriage ritual and prayers and to traditional Jewish views on cohabitation. Our hope is that congregations will develop programs exploring these traditions as congregants and clergy create additional, meaningful cohabitation rituals.

A Blessing for Love[7]

Today we sanctify the union of _____ and _____ , and we recall another sacred beginning, that of creation itself. God created the heavens, and earth was formed. Life was granted on the land and in the sea. Genesis tells of the

---

6. Adapted from Richard F. Address, "Creating Sacred Scenarios," article submitted for publication to *Journal of Gerontological Social Work*.
7. By Rabbi Benjamin David, from an assignment for "The Changing Jewish Family," taught by Richard F. Address at Hebrew Union College–Jewish Institute of Religion, New York, NY, Spring 2003.

sanctity of human companionship, of togetherness in the holy union of two people. In sanctifying this union today, we foster the long-standing emphasis on togetherness. _____ and _____ have found one another and now seek to come together. May their union animate the divine in each of them and help the other to grow in the likeness of God.

Do you, _____, promise to support and comfort _____ , providing him/her with love and compassion, from this day forward? *(Repeat for both individuals.)*

May the union of _____ and _____ be for a blessing, and may they find health, love, and happiness in their days together.

Amen.

A Commitment Blessing[8]

Today we celebrate the loving commitment of _____ and _____ to each other, and we share in their joy.

In the Song of Songs we read אֲנִי לְדוֹדִי וְדוֹדִי לִי (*Ani l'dodi v'dodi li*), "I am my beloved's, and my beloved is mine." This represents not only God's relationship with Israel, but also the commitment that is shared between _____ and

_____.

Love lives as long as the human heart beats, as long as we draw breath. The soul reaches out to another, recognizing a kindred spirit, a receptive companion to share life's vicissitudes. Age is meaningless, for the mysteries of the heart know no temporal boundaries.

Today we acknowledge their love for each other, and bless their commitment:

> May they be healthy and lead productive lives.
> May they find sustenance in their relationship.
> May they find enjoyment in each other.
> May their physical presence strengthen their spiritual growth.
> May they nurture their fragility and rely on their strengths.
> May their days be full, and inundated with love.
> Amen.

Spouses in New Relationships Due to Dementia

Another suggestion for new rituals and ceremonies is, perhaps, the most difficult. It stems from the increasing challenges that are presented in dealing with the issue of a loved one who is institutionalized with Alzheimer's, suffers from dementia, or is in a persistent vegetative state.

The scenario may be familiar to some. It is the well spouse who comes to the clergy-person to seek counsel. He or she has met someone, and that someone provides a sense of comfort and intimacy (which may or may not be sexual in nature). There is no talk of abandoning the spouse who is ill. However, there is the argument that, given the nature and duration of the illness, should not the well spouse be free to find someone with whom he or she can share life and find support?

---

8. Adapted from a service performed by Marcia Goren Weser at an assisted-living facility in San Antonio, Texas.

The rituals for cohabitation, therefore, could be supplemented with additional prayers recognizing the emotional strain that one faces when his or her loved one is suffering from dementia. The well spouse is comforted in knowing that the union is receiving a special blessing, while at the same time the spouse with dementia is not being abandoned.

In many of the pilot Sacred Aging workshops conducted by the Department of Jewish Family Concerns, this scenario arose with astounding frequency. What seems to be true is that this is a very real issue for many of our congregants and, given the longevity revolution, may become a reality for many more in the years ahead. The question was always raised as to the wisdom of having this issue discussed by the congregation. Should the caring community provide educational programs that would seek to raise this issue of the well spouse who seeks emotional, physical, or spiritual comfort from another? Should a congregation develop a document that would give "permission" for those who find themselves in this position to be permitted to seek such comfort from someone other than their spouse? Or should this remain a private matter to be discussed between the congregant and the rabbi? What is clear is that the issue is real. There are serious issues here that go to the heart of relationships, needs and wants, and one's view of self and family. We urge the discussion of this issue. We need to send the message that our communities understand that new life stages have created new demands for the embrace of community.

A look at the impact of ritual in the area of sexuality and intimacy can be obtained from "With Eyes Undimmed and Vigor Unabated: Sexuality and Older Adults," by Richard F. Address (*CCAR Journal*, Fall 2001, pp. 58–67).

O Source of Healing[9]

Our God and God of all generations, in our great need we pour out our hearts to You. The days and weeks of suffering are hard to endure. In our struggle, let us feel that You are near, a presence whose care enfolds us. Rouse in us the strength to overcome fear and anxiety, and brighten our spirits with the assurance of Your love. Strengthen and encourage us. Let your spirit be with our loved one, _____, and give us strength through these days, to continue our lives with loving-kindness and joyfulness.

בָּרוּךְ אַתָּה יְיָ, רוֹפֵא הַחוֹלִים.

Baruch atah Adonai, rofei hacholim.

We praise You, O God, the Source of healing.

Sustain Our Love[10]

We are grateful, O God, for the gift of life and for the sustaining powers that You have implanted within Your creatures. Be with _____, our loved one, through these days, months, and years of illness. Implant within him/her the courage and fortitude he/she needs to endure weakness, loss of memory, and pain. Help us to

---

9. Adapted and revised from *On the Doorposts of Your House*, p. 152. The prayer can be said by the couple together, or it can be revised so that it is said by the caregiving spouse.
10. Ibid.

continue to find ways to show our love and concern for him/her, so that we both may be an influence for good in his/her time of need.

And may all others who suffer illness of body or mind know that You are with them, giving them strength of spirit as they struggle to recover. May their afflictions soon be ended, and may they return in health to family and friends.

בָּרוּךְ אַתָּה יְיָ, רוֹפֵא הַחוֹלִים.

Baruch atah Adonai, rofei hacholim.

We praise You, O God, the Source of healing.

Marking a Significant Transition

Upon Retirement

This ceremony is divided into several readings and may all be read by one leader or by several people. It can be said during a special ceremony at the synagogue or even at a gathering of people celebrating the retirement (such as a retirement party). The leader can be a clergy member or even a coworker.

The Retirement of a Friend[11]

Leader: Retirement is cause for both celebration and reflection. In coming together for this ceremony in honor of _____'s retirement, we create a sacred time and place to honor his/her contributions and to support him/her in making this significant life transition.

Retiree: Jewish life has much to teach us about time and transitions. Not only major life transitions are acknowledged in our tradition, but even the setting of the sun each evening is cause for thanks and for taking a few moments to notice the passing of a day and the appearance of the stars. Like the stars, which can only be seen in the dark, some elements of life shine brighter when other elements are no longer present. Let retirement be for me an ending and a beginning, and may I find many parts of my life shining brightly in the time to come.

Congregation/Group:

> We are loved by an unending love.
> We are embraced by arms that find us
> Even when we are hidden from ourselves.
> We are touched by fingers that soothe us
> Even when we are too proud for soothing.
> We are counseled by voices that guide us
> Even when we are too embittered to hear.
> We are loved by an unending love.

All: Amen.

---

11. Anonymous.

These next two prayers are intended to be recited by the retiree. Again, they would be appropriate to recite during a service at a congregation or even before family or coworkers at a ceremony commemorating the retirement.

A Retirement Wish[12]

Now I have precious time to give to those I love, to family and friends. I pray for insight and a warm heart; let me be with them when they need me, let me respond when they call to me. And let me use my leisure to explore new worlds of thought and feeling, or to rediscover old ones. Now I can study my heritage of Torah and Judaism, savor the beauties of nature and art, find new meaning and inspiration in the books of life. Let the passage of time continually deepen with me the spirit of knowledge and reverence for life.

And let me never lose that sense of wonder that the presence of your creation stirs within me and that beckons me to greet each day with zest and eager welcome. Thus will I bring blessing to many in the years to come.

Amen.

Continuing the Journey[13]

Tonight I need to pause for a moment to ask, What is it that I am retiring from in this phase of life? A specific job in a specific location with a specific salary and benefits. But certainly I am not retiring from creativity, drive, spirit, interests, certainly not retiring from life!

By giving to others, loving and sharing, let me continue to find meaning in everything I do. Let me recognize God in all of my deeds, so that I may come to know the timelessness of my soul and grow closer to God. The very fact that God has granted me a single additional day of life means that I have not yet concluded my mission in life, and that there is still much to achieve in this world.

Amen.

Moving into a Retirement Home

This beautiful ceremony can be led by a layperson or a clergy member. It takes place at a retirement home or any other assisted-living facility. The traditional *V'ahavta* and *Sh'ma* prayers are incorporated in the ritual, giving concrete meaning to the Jewish mandate of remembering God's commandments "on the doorposts of your house." The ritual includes not only the resident's family and friends, but the staff at the residence as well. Giving the staff the opportunity to participate in a ceremony commemorating such a significant transition—in this case hanging up a mezuzah—sends the message that the work they do is special and meaningful.

---

12. Adapted from "A Service of Renewal to Honor Those Newly Retired Among Us," prepared by Betsy Dobrick of Congregation B'nai Israel in Boca Raton, Florida.
13. Ibid.

Affixing a Mezuzah upon Moving into a Nursing Home[14]

Leader: Today we consecrate a moment of transition. In the journey of life, this transition is a significant milestone. Feelings of hope and of fear, of anticipation and of anxiety, of sorrow and perhaps of relief accompany this transition. Embarking on this new phase of the journey, we reflect on the progression of life. We contemplate the changes and the challenges yet to be faced.

With hearts full of emotion, we turn to the words of Jewish tradition, seeking faith in the midst of uncertainty.

Group:

God is my light and my help;
Whom shall I fear?
The Eternal is the strength of my life;
Of whom shall I be afraid?

שְׁמַע יִשְׂרָאֵל, יְהוָה אֱלֹהֵינוּ, יְהוָה אֶחָד!

Sh'ma Yisrael, Adonai Eloheinu, Adonai Echad!

Hear, O Israel, the Eternal is our God, the Eternal is One!

בָּרוּךְ שֵׁם כְּבוֹד מַלְכוּתוֹ לְעוֹלָם וָעֶד.

Baruch shem k'vod malchuto l'olam va-ed.

Blessed is the name of God's glorious kingdom forever and ever.

Leader:

וְאָהַבְתָּ אֵת יְהוָה אֱלֹהֶיךָ בְּכָל־לְבָבְךָ וּבְכָל־נַפְשְׁךָ וּבְכָל־מְאֹדֶךָ:

V'ahavta eit Adonai Elohecha, b'chol l'vavcha,
uv'chol nafsh'cha, uv'chol m'odecha.

You shall love the Eternal your God with all your heart, with all your soul,
and with all your strength.

Resident (or family member): May I respond in love and in trust to the will of the Creator of Life, with all my heart, with all my soul, and with all my strength.

Leader:

וְהָיוּ הַדְּבָרִים הָאֵלֶּה אֲשֶׁר אָנֹכִי מְצַוְּךָ הַיּוֹם עַל־לְבָבֶךָ:

V'hayu hadvarim ha-eileh, asher anochi m'tzavcha hayom al l'vavecha.

These words, which I command you this day, shall be upon your heart.

---

14. Adapted from a ceremony by Cary Kozberg, in *A Heart of Wisdom: Making the Jewish Journey from Midlife through the Elder Years*, ed. Susan Berrin (Woodstock, VT: Jewish Lights Publishing, 1997).

Resident (or family member): When my spirit darkens, may I daily take to heart the promise of the Ancient of Days: "I am with you in your distress. I will not forsake you."

Leader:

וְשִׁנַּנְתָּם לְבָנֶיךָ וְדִבַּרְתָּ בָּם בְּשִׁבְתְּךָ בְּבֵיתֶךָ וּבְלֶכְתְּךָ בַדֶּרֶךְ וּבְשָׁכְבְּךָ וּבְקוּמֶךָ׃

V'shinantam l'vanecha v'dibarta bam, b'shivt'cha b'veitecha,
uv'lecht'cha vaderech, uv'shochb'cha uv'kumecha.

Teach them faithfully to your children, speaking of them when in
your home, when you lie down, and when you rise up.

Resident (or family member): Even in physical frailty, let me retain strength of spirit. May my life maintain its sense of purpose, and may I be an exemplar of courage and hope to my family and friends.

Leader:

וּקְשַׁרְתָּם לְאוֹת עַל־יָדֶךָ וְהָיוּ לְטֹטָפֹת בֵּין עֵינֶיךָ׃

Uk'shartam l'ot al yadecha v'hayu l'totafot bein einecha.

Bind them as a sign upon your arm, and let them be symbols between your eyes.

Resident (or family member): May Divine caring always be evident to me. May God's mercy always be present to me. May God's strength inspire me to keep my body energized and my mind active, and may the Source of Life always watch over my spirit, even when it departs this world.

Leader:

וּכְתַבְתָּם עַל־מְזֻזוֹת בֵּיתֶךָ וּבִשְׁעָרֶיךָ׃

Uch'tavtam al m'zuzot beitecha uvisharecha.

Write them upon the doorposts of your house and upon your gates.

Resident (or family member): May the Divine Presence, symbolized by this mezuzah, be felt in this room by all who enter. May that Presence continue to sustain me, as it has sustained those who came before me, and as it will sustain those who will come after me.

(Affix the mezuzah and say:)

בָּרוּךְ אַתָּה יְיָ, אֱלֹהֵינוּ מֶלֶךְ הָעוֹלָם אֲשֶׁר קִדְּשָׁנוּ בְּמִצְוֹתָיו וְצִוָּנוּ לִקְבּוֹעַ מְזוּזָה׃

Baruch atah Adonai, Ehloheinu Melech haolam,
asher kid'shanu b'mitzvotav v'tzivanu likboa m'zuzah.

Blessed are You, Eternal our God, Ruler of the universe,
who has sanctified us with Your commandments,
and commanded us to affix the mezuzah.

Staff: On behalf of the entire staff, we want to welcome you, _____, to our _____ (name of facility) family. We hope that the adjustment for you and your family will be an easy one, and we promise to meet your needs and concerns to the best of our ability.

As you join our family, may you be blessed and sustained by these ancient words:

Leader:

יְבָרֶכְךָ יְיָ וְיִשְׁמְרֶךָ.

Y'varech'cha Adonai v'yishm'recha.

May God bless you and keep you.

יָאֵר יְיָ פָּנָיו אֵלֶיךָ וִיחֻנֶּךָ.

Ya-eir Adonai panav eilecha vichunecha.

May God's face shine upon you, and may God always be gracious to you.

יִשָּׂא יְיָ פָּנָיו אֵלֶיךָ וְיָשֵׂם לְךָ שָׁלוֹם.

Yisa Adonai panav eilecha v'yasem l'cha shalom.

May God's face shine upon you and grant you peace.
And let us all say: Amen.

Facing Challenging Times

Removing the Wedding Band Following the Year of Mourning

Removing the wedding band after mourning a spouse can be a heart-wrenching experience. However, if the following ritual accompanies the act, the surviving spouse is allowed an outlet to express his or her feelings. Both of these prayers can be recited in front of family and friends, either at home or during a service at a congregation. The first of these prayers emerged from the request of a congregant to his rabbi following the year of mourning. The member and the rabbi worked to develop a ritual of closure that spoke to the member. The second prayer emerged from one of the pilot project discussions that took place as the Sacred Aging project developed. These are meant to be examples of what some people may need to move on. Obviously, these are intensely personal choices that need to be discussed and worked through with clergy.

With This Ring[15]

With this ring I was betrothed to you,
According to the laws of Moses, Miriam, and Israel.

Ecclesiastes teaches me that there is a time for everything,
Especially for birth and for death.

---

15. Adapted from a prayer by Barry E. Pitegoff of Temple Israel, Tallahassee, Florida.

From our heritage I learned the importance of reaffirming our faith
Even at the most difficult times,
Even when in the Valley of the Shadow of Death.

With the removal of this ring, I acknowledge again
That I am losing your companionship.
But the memories and love will always remain
Dear to my heart.

May they continue as an inspiration to me
And to those you touched.
May they remain a blessing,
And may we always praise God
For the gifts of life and patience,
And for the righteous judgments made.

God asks that we walk in the way of Torah.
May that continue to be my will.

Amen.

This Precious Ring[16]

This precious ring you slipped on my finger as we stood under our chuppah
I took to my heart as a continuous circle of love.
It remained a symbol of our unity as we held our babies,
celebrated our milestones, and soothed our hurts.
A witness to all of our married days, it was once new and shining.
With the passing of years the color deepened and warmed,
As did the exquisiteness of our life together.
Now I am without you and I must move to another way of living.

I must begin a new life.

As I remove this circle of love,
I know it is not easy to let go
And surrender into memory what once was
And can no longer be.
As I heal and go forward,
I will always be strengthened by a life we cherished,
And that part of my heart that is forever yours.

Amen.

---

16. Adapted from a prayer by Marlene Levenson of Congregation Beth Am, Los Altos Hills, California.

Completing the Year of Mourning

These two prayers can be read by a widow or widower marking the one-year anniversary of the death of a loved one. They can be read when the surviving spouse lights the *yahrzeit* candle in his or her home.

It May Be[17]

It may be so with us, that in the dark
When we have done with time and wander space,
Some meeting of the blind may strike a spark,
And to death's empty mansion give a grace.

It may be that the loosened soul may find
Some delight in living without limbs,
Bodiless joy of flesh-untrammeled mind,
Peace like a sky where starlit spirit swims.

It may be that the million cells of sense,
Loosed from their seventy years' adhesion, pass
Each to some joy of changed experience,
Weight in the earth or glory in the grass;

It may be that we cease; we cannot tell.
Even if we cease, life is a miracle.

It is a Fearful Thing[18]

It is a fearful thing to love what death can touch.
A fearful thing to love, hope, dream: to be—
To be, and Oh! to lose.

A thing for fools, this, a holy thing, a holy thing to love.

For your life has lived in me, your laugh once lifted me,
your word was a gift to me.

To remember this brings painful joy.

It is a human thing, love, a holy thing,
to love what death has touched.

---

17. Anonymous.
18. Anonymous.

Summary of Ritual Topics

"Through the way a community prays, it defines who it is, whence it comes, and how it chooses to express its own individuality."[19] The ethics of a community are displayed in how we choose to pray as a community. The rituals included above reflect the changing values of our society. They are meant to bring comfort and solace to those who may be in mourning or are hurting, and festiveness and joy to those who may be coming into new and exciting phases of their lives. In other words, they define who we are, what we care about, and what we hold to be valuable and sacred.

This chapter contains only some of the ideas that were developed for rituals that pertain to the aging process. Other ideas wait for your consideration and, perhaps, their creation through programming at your congregation. Below is a summary of the issues that were most requested in ritual creation workshops held at numerous congregations.[20]

The central question raised by this summary is, which rites of passage do you consider to be most sacred? Answering this question involves personal introspection. Not every ritual will be particularly meaningful for every congregant, because most rituals are developed based upon personal experience. However, we hope that if any of the events described below resonate with you because of feelings of sorrow, joy, sadness, or exultation that you may have felt, then you will consider working with your congregation in creating a meaningful and moving ritual.

1. Celebrating special moments
   - On passing Jewish tradition to children and grandchildren
   - Celebrations of daily miracles of life
   - Giving thanks for a fulfilling and joyful life
   - Renewal of marriage vows
   - On the anniversary of becoming bar/bat mitzvah
   - On distributing heirlooms of one who has died
   - Upon becoming a grandparent/great-grandparent
   - Family reunions
   - Honoring older members of the congregation
   - On becoming an organ donor/receiving an organ donation
   - Senior confirmation/bar or bat mitzvah
   - Returning to school
   - Returning to the study of Torah as an adult
   - Special birthdays
   - Recovery from illness/surgery
2. Marking a significant transition
   - Moving into an assisted-living or nursing home facility
   - Removing the mezuzah from the home upon moving
   - Acknowledging the past before a special life-altering event (i.e., prior to a child's wedding)
   - Acknowledging the support of family in making a decision regarding a change in life

---

19. Lawrence A. Hoffman, *Beyond the Text: A Holistic Approach to Liturgy* (Bloomington, IN: Indiana University Press, 1987), p. 58.
20. The Jewish Council for the Aging created a document entitled "Readings and Rituals for the Joys, Challenges, and Transitions of Senior Adulthood." A few of the topics listed here, as well as the categorization of those topics, were adopted from that document. To request a copy, contact the Jewish Council for the Aging at (301) 255-4200.

- When older adults move in with children
- Giving up a driver's license
- When children leave the home
- Discharge from military service
- Upon retirement

3. Facing challenging times
   - On dealing with loneliness
   - Dealing with the loss of adult children
   - Upon learning that one has a life-threatening disease
   - Giving support for a widow/widower
   - Upon needing a caregiver
   - Dealing with a serious illness
   - Serious medical changes
   - Onset of menopause
   - Letting go at the end of life

The new rituals presented in this chapter "speak to a changing older adult reality. Longevity, mobility, wellness, and a heightened awareness of the mystery that is life have produced a fascinating dialogue as to new ritual possibilities." The longevity revolution has produced a sincere awareness of the need to celebrate and sanctify life in meaningful, ritualistic ways.[21]

Rituals are perhaps the most concrete way to affirm the models by which we choose to live our lives. Being old does not mean that we have ceased our quest to sanctify life. Indeed, our longevity demands that we explore new ways to show the deep love and respect for the relationships in our lives.

> May this time be a beginning of renewed blessings.
> Blessings of goodness, blessings of joy,
> Peace and kindness, friendship and love,
> Creativity, strength, serenity,
> Fulfillment and dignity,
> Satisfaction, success and sustenance,
> Physical health and radiance.
>
> May truth and justice guide our acts.
> May compassion temper our lives,
> That we may blossom as we age,
> And become our sweetest selves.
>
> May it be so in our eyes and in the eyes of God.[22]

---

21. Richard F. Address, "Spirituality and Aging," *NCJW Journal*, Summer 1999, p. 13.
22. From "A Service of Renewal to Honor Those Newly Retired Among Us."

Additional Resources

Books

Brener, Anne. *Mourning and Mitzvah*. Woodstock, VT: Jewish Lights Publishing, 1993.

Falk, Marcia. *The Book of Blessings*. San Francisco: HarperSanFrancisco, 1996.

Ihara, Toni. *Living Together: A Legal Guide for Unmarried Couples*. Berkeley, CA: Nolo, 2004.

Kozberg, Cary. "Saving Broken Tablets: Planning for the Spiritual Needs of Jews in Long-Term Care Facilities" in *A Heart of Wisdom: Making the Jewish Journey from Midlife through the Elder Years*, ed. Susan Berrin. Woodstock, VT: Jewish Lights Publishing, 1997.

Sherman, Andrea, and Marsha Weiner. *Transitional Keys: A Guidebook—Rituals to Improve Quality of Life for Older Adults*. Dobbs Ferry, NY: Transitional Keys, 2004.

Solot, Dorian, and Marshall Miller. *Unmarried to Each Other: The Essential Guide to Living Together as an Unmarried Couple*. Emeryville, CA: Avalon, 2002.

Liturgical References

"A Service of Renewal to Honor Those Newly Retired Among Us," by Congregation B'nai Israel, Boca Raton, Florida. (Contact the Union for Reform Judaism, Department of Jewish Family Concerns at 212-650-4294, or by e-mail at **JFC@urj.org**).

Stern, Chaim, ed. *On the Doorpost of Your House: Prayers and Ceremonies for the Jewish Home*. New York: CCAR Press, 1994.

Web Sites

www.transitionalkeys.org: Transitional Keys offers ways of bringing the power of ritual to support the aging.

www.creativeaging.org: The National Center for Creative Aging offers programming for elders to creatively express issues relating to aging.

www.spiritualeldering.org: The Spiritual Eldering Institute trains lay leaders and clergy to cultivate the experiences of elders into blessings and rituals.

www.unmarried.org: The Alternatives to Marriage Project provides information and links to sites for cohabiting couples.

www.nolo.com: For legal issues associated with cohabiting.

4

Making Sacred Decisions: Medical Technology and Jewish Values

Sanctity of life means that man is a partner, not a sovereign, that life is a trust, not a property.
To exist as a human being is to assist the divine.
Abraham Joshua Heschel,
The Insecurity of Freedom: Essays on Human Existence, p. 49

The impact of medical technology has contributed greatly to the revolution in longevity. It is a fact that many in our congregations will be faced with difficult choices, especially as life's end nears. Likewise, chronic illness will impact increasing numbers of us, illnesses that may also require us to make difficult decisions.

We suggest that congregations regularly schedule workshops, classes, or special educational seminars that teach members how to approach decision making from within the framework of Jewish values, history, and texts. Many congregations have begun to do this. As the number of older adults increases and caregiving concerns multiply, it becomes important for our congregations to make these sessions a regular feature of their continuing educational program.

Some congregations have run multi-session workshops featuring clergy, elder care lawyers, insurance experts, local funeral directors, and so on. These sessions are devoted to educating the congregation as to Jewish tradition, local, state, and provincial laws regarding advance directives and powers of attorney, funeral and mourning customs, and more. *The importance of having these sessions on a regular basis cannot be overstated. Family dynamics change regularly, so there is always a need for regular education to teach and discuss these most powerful of issues.* Some congregations have developed their own guides to end-of-life practices (contact the URJ Department of Jewish Family Concerns for samples). In many cases, congregations will distribute the publication *A Time to Prepare* (URJ Press), the Union's guide on advance directives, ethical wills, rituals, personal life data, and responsa that deal with end-of-life decision making. Likewise, many congregations in developing these programs make use of physicians, ethicists, nurses, and social workers who are members of the congregation and who are honored to be asked to teach what they know to adults and youth. These are valuable resources within every congregation, and congregations who make use of these resources report high levels of satisfaction and mutual learning. For an example of a multi-session program, see "Honor Your Father and Mother: A Time to Prepare" on pages 40–41.

The following outlines a congregation-based workshop on decision making in light of emerging medical technology. It has been used in several congregations as the Sacred Aging project was developing. It presents a brief look at key texts that inform Judaism and medicine, introduces contemporary issues that impact how people make decisions, and concludes with a theory of decision making that is drawn from the texts. It can be used with *A Time to Prepare*. There are many additional resources that can be used to create a small library for participants who have an interest in the link between Judaism and medicine. We include some of these resources at the end of this chapter.

Sample Workshop on Making Sacred Decisions

Theological Foundation: Judaism as a Holistic Medical-Spiritual System

Judaism understands that there is a fundamental relationship between humankind and God. There is a sacred partnership between God and physician.

Maimonides represents a **holistic** approach to medicine. He reflects Judaism's acceptance that there is a distinct link between the mind and the body and the soul. All are interconnected, and in treating someone, all must be taken into account. This approach may differ from a more "Western" approach to medicine, and the following text raises interesting questions on the role of alternative approaches to treating a person:

> In his *Guide for the Perplexed*, Maimonides describes the general objective of Torah law as the well being of body and the well being of the soul. Bodily well being is established by removing violence from our midst, eliminating the pattern of everyone doing as he or she pleases, and by teaching good morals that produce a good social context. The well being of the soul is only attained after the well being of the body has been secured. Maimonides argues that one who suffers from hunger, thirst, heat or cold is incapable of grasping an idea, even if communicated by others, and is even less likely to reach conclusions autonomously. However, if a person is in possession of the first perfection, i.e., well being of the body, that individual is able to acquire the second perfection, i.e., well being of the soul. This is the intent of Torah commandments in their entirety, to effect perfection of the body and the soul. In other words, the Torah is vitally concerned with the human psychological state, the state of the human psyche. All these commandments of the Torah become, in a sense, meta-clinical directives for meaningful living, for the good of humankind.[1]

Texts from the Tradition That Give Permission for Humankind to "Heal"

Judaism derives its sanctions for actions by examining sacred texts and interpreting them. The following are key texts that helped shape Jewish tradition's approach to sanctioning

---

1. Fred Rosner, *Moses Maimonides: Physician, Scientist, and Philosopher*, ed. Samuel S. Kotteck (Northvale, NJ: Jason Aronson, 1993), p. 140.

humankind's ability to, as the Talmud says, "fly in the face of Providence," thus seeking to combat illness.

Notice that the goal of some of these texts is to restore or provide us with an ability to stand in relationship with God (again the importance of this fundamental relationship between humankind and God). Likewise, Judaism understands that we pray for "healing," and not cure. It is possible, the tradition says, to be "healed" (psychologically and spiritually) and not be "cured" of a disease. This speaks to the holistic approach and is present often in hospice work. (See the URJ resolution "Compassion and Comfort Care at the End of Life," adopted by the UAHC General Assembly in 1995 and available at **www.urj.org /docs/reso/**.)

Prayer Book

- "Heal us and we shall be healed, save us and we shall be saved. Grant full healing to our wounds, our illness, our pain. Blessed are You, Eternal, Healer of the sick" (from the *Amidah*).
- "Blessed are You Eternal One, our God, Sovereign of the universe. With divine wisdom You have made our bodies, combining veins, arteries, and vital organs into a finely balanced network. Wondrous Maker and Sustainer of life, were one of them to fail—how well we are aware!—we would lack the strength to stand in life before You. Blessed are You, Eternal One, Source of our health and strength" (from the morning service).

Additional Proof Texts

- God as "healer," *rof'echa*: "If you will heed the Eternal your God diligently, doing what is upright in God's sight, giving ear to God's commandments and keeping all God's laws, then I will not bring upon you any of the diseases that I brought upon the Egyptians, for I the Eternal am your healer" (Exodus 15:26).
- "When individuals quarrel and one strikes the other with stone or fist, and the victim does not die but has to take to bed: if that victim then gets up and walks outdoors upon a staff, the assailant shall go unpunished—except for paying for the idleness [time lost] and the cure" (Exodus 21:18–19). The Hebrew root for "healing" is repeated at the end of the verse (*v'rapo y'rapei*), thus giving rise to the interpretation that healing is of major concern.
- "Do not stand by the blood of your neighbor" (Leviticus 19:16). This mandates that we must intervene, especially when life is at stake.
- The obligation to intervene is also reflected in the following: "The Torah gave permission to heal. Moreover, this is a religious obligation and is included in the category of saving life; and if a physician withholds services, it is considered as shedding blood" (*Shulchan Aruch, Yoreh Dei-ah* 336:1).
- "If you see your fellow Israelite's ox or sheep gone astray, do not ignore it; you must take it back to your peer. If your fellow Israelite does not live near you or you do not know who [the owner] is, you shall bring it home and it shall remain with you until your peer claims it; then you shall **cause it to be returned to him**" (Deuteronomy 22:1–2). Maimonides takes the last part of the verse to mean that when one loses one's health, it is incumbent to do what must be done to cause that health to be returned. Many scholars of Judaism and medicine see this interpretation as raising intervention to a divine mandate.

- "It was taught: How do we know that saving a life supersedes the laws of Shabbat? Rabbi Y'hudah said in the name of Sh'muel: For it is written: 'You shall keep My laws and My rules, by the pursuit of which human beings shall live' (Leviticus 18:5)" (Babylonian Talmud, *Yoma* 85b). Commandments are given for life, to live by them, and not die by them (see also Babylonian Talmud, *Sanhedrin* 74a). From this we understand that a basic value of Judaism is that in order to save a life, we may violate even the laws of Shabbat.

Fundamental Ethic: The Dignity and Sanctity of Human Life

From a look at texts, we can determine the existence of a fundamental ethic that guides us in making decisions: The dignity and sanctity of human life and the preservation of that human life in dignity and in sanctity.

The following questions must then be raised:

- How do we define what "dignity" and "sanctity" are in light of current medical technology?
- Are there absolute definitions of these terms, or are there "gray" areas?

In attempting to apply the fundamental ethic of Judaism to the real world of our people today, our decisions will be impacted by several issues. These "wild cards" come to be factored into each decision and reflect the individual and the family dynamic that embraces the individual.

The "Wild Cards" that Impact Decision Making and the Application of the Fundamental Ethic

Autonomy

- Autonomy is a major issue for contemporary Jews: the conflict between the belief that this is "my body" and "my life" versus the belief that "my body and my life are a gift from God and I do *not* have ultimate control."
- The myth of control: Look at the High Holy Day prayer *Un'taneh tokef*, which reminds us that ultimate control of life and death rests in a power beyond us.
- Discuss the issue of autonomy (a peculiar American issue?) in relationship to self, community, and God. Consider one interpretation of the *Akeidah,* which reminds us that sometimes to be truly free we must accept restraints (binding).

Technology

- The neutrality of technology: It is how we choose to use it that makes the difference, thus our need to "educate for choices" (Deuteronomy 30).
- Information does not always equal knowledge. The information age in which we live leads some to see a "promiscuity of information." Technology has given us many gifts; however, just because we "can" do something does not always means that we "should" do something.
- Judaism reminds us (Genesis 1 and 2, as well as Psalm 8) that we have "power and dominion" over our world. In other words, we have been given a mandate to see in research and advancing technology the possibility for developing tools that may honor the fundamen-

tal ethic (e.g., stem cell research). The challenge is educating for choices and sanctity and life.

Spirituality

- In making decisions, how do we see God?
- When we go to a doctor, he or she takes a medical history. Should your congregation develop a "spiritual history" form that would allow members to grapple with their spirituality in light of their own health care and religious beliefs that may impact treatment? (See "A Sample Form for Creating a Spiritual History" on pages 80–82.)
- See the synagogue as a source of educating for decision making. In this, we see another distinction between the scientific approach and the religious approach. Most of us see issues in terms of "how", we can approach them, what treatments are best, and so on. The religious questions begin with the "why" of the issue.
- Discuss the idea of the *shomeir*, the caretaker (see chapter 2). Benjamin Freedman approaches caretaking from the concept of stewardship, which means that when making decisions for someone else, the caretaker must do no harm and make decisions that ensure that the other person's wishes are honored and respected, even if they contradict the caretaker's own wishes. (For a challenging approach to this subject see Benjamin Freedman, *Duty and Healing: Foundations of Jewish Bioethic* [New York: Routledge Press, 1999].)

A Theory of Decision Making

How do we take the fundamental ethic, derived from texts and influenced by the wild cards of contemporary culture, and apply it to making sacred decisions?

1. What is the Jewish value we are looking at?
   a. In end-of-life issues this value may often be the value of life and the tradition's understanding of *pikuach nefesh* as the most important value, so important that in order to save a life we may violate even the laws of Shabbat.
   b. This raises, as does the fundamental ethic, the question as to whether "life" is an absolute value in Judaism, that is, are we mandated to save life in each and every case, no matter what?
2. Context
   a. Judaism teaches us that we look at the case before us. We seek to apply the value to the specific case. No two cases may be exactly alike (note that here is where "wild cards" really impact).
   b. Are there, for example, Jewish legal categories that can serve as guidelines or boundaries up to which one set of actions is mandated and beyond which there is a change in emphasis in how we *may* treat a person? Legal terms such as *goseis* and *t'reifah* are now valuable in defining how far one *may* go in extraordinary treatment. Here the discussions regarding quality of life and prolonging life versus delaying death are most relevant.
      (1) *Goseis*: a moribund patient whose death is imminent (usually, in tradition, seen as three days—from interpretations of the *Shulchan Aruch*). Given the "wild card" of technology, how do we understand *goseis* in our world? Discuss the permissibility of removing extraordinary treatments. When does treatment prolong life or just delay death?

(2) *T'reifah*: someone who is "marked for death." Examples are people living with serious, terminal illness but not anywhere near the end of life. Do different methods of treatment apply?

c. How and where does the issue of quality of life come into play in these areas, especially given the "wild cards" of autonomy and technology and personal spirituality?

3. Choice

a. We apply the value to the context of the specific case, taking into consideration the impact of the various "wild cards," and from that we can be shown an appropriate choice.

b. Look at Deuteronomy 30 again: God offers the choice between life and death, blessing and curse, good and evil. Again, it is necessary to educate for choices.

c. The power of ritual: How can ritual be a supportive presence in these moments? Consider traditional rituals in the context of end of life and how they can remain relevant.

The theory of making sacred decisions, therefore, involves value, context, and choice.

In making decisions in light of medical technology, we understand that we are rooted in a holistic system that sees a fundamental ethic emerging from our interpretations of Jewish texts. We then apply that ethic to the "wild cards" of autonomy, technology, and spirituality; we apply those to the value we are dealing with and the context of the case; and thus we can be guided to an appropriate Jewish choice. Often in this day and age, these choices are not between right and wrong or good and bad, but between different shades of sadness.

The following quote helps illustrate the power of making these decisions:

The quantity of life is in the hands of God, the quality of life is in our hands only.[2]

Sample Form for Creating a Spiritual History

A suggestion for another educational/action program is to develop a congregation-based form to assess members' spiritual beliefs. The goal of this, other than creating discussion and study, would be to provide members with a tool to give to their physicians in case of need. This is reflective of the Jewish holistic approach to treating the person. The following was developed by Rabbi Todd A. Markley while a student at Hebrew Union College–Jewish Institute of Religion in New York. It was created as a result of discussions in a class on sacred aging. This is presented as a model for your examination, and we invite you to adapt it to your congregation.

Name: _____

Religious affiliation: _____ Denomination: _____

Congregation/location: _____

Name of clergy person: _____ Phone: _____

---

2. Rabbi Max Ardst, in Philip Goodman, *Rosh Hashanah Anthology* (Philadelphia: Jewish Publication Society, 1973), p. 95.

Name and relation of primary caregiver(s): _____

Name and contact of primary care physician: _____

Religious Affiliation

A1. Were you raised in the same religion with which you now affiliate? If not, what other traditions have you practiced?

A2. Have you always been affiliated with the same denomination with which you are now affiliated? If not, with which other(s) have you been affiliated in the past?

A3. Has your religious community been helpful to you in the past? How?

A4. What type of support might you desire from your religious community in times of illness (e.g., visits, calls, prayers, rituals)?

Personal Religious Beliefs and Practices

B1. Are there Jewish teachings that provide helpful insight into matters of health and illness for you? If so, what are they?

B2. Are there Jewish messages about health and illness, life and death, that do not work for you or that you find incongruous with your own sensibilities? If so, what are they?

B3. Do you believe in God? Describe that belief and your relationship with God.

B4. What role does God play, however you understand God, in your health and well-being?

B5. What aspects of your personal, spiritual, or religious life do you find helpful to you in illness or in difficult times (e.g., prayer, ritual, meditation)?

B6. Are there specific prayers with which you have a personal connection or in which you find strength or hope?

B7. Have your religious beliefs changed over time? If so, how?

B8. When you are, someday, approaching the end of life, will reciting the *Vidui* (deathbed confessional) or the *Sh'ma* be important for you? Would you want either prayer recited for you if you were unable to do so?

B9. Are there any Jewish ritual practices that the hospital staff should know about to make your stay more comfortable (e.g., dietary restrictions/kashrut, prayer needs, ritual dress)?

B10. During a hospital stay, would you be interested in speaking to the hospital's pastoral care staff regardless of their religious affiliation, or would you prefer only to be visited by Jewish clergy?

Other Sources of Spiritual Well-Being

C1. Where do you find strength, comfort, and support (from whom and in what setting)?

C2. What helps to keep you going in difficult times?

C3. What do you need in order to be at peace?

Potential Impediments to Spiritual Health

D1. Is it likely that your illness will bring up unresolved issues that will interfere with your spiritual well-being (e.g., family conflicts)?

D2. Are there aspects of your life that will go unattended, causing you distress during a prolonged illness (e.g., pets that need care; community, job, or family responsibilities)?

D3. Are there any specific items from home that will be important for you to have with you during a hospital stay and that your caregivers can provide for you?

Additional Resources

Books

Address, Richard F., ed. *A Time to Prepare: A Practical Guide for Individuals and Families in Determining a Jewish Approach to Making Personal Arrangements, Establishing the Limits of Medical Care, and Embracing Rituals at the End of Life*, rev. ed. New York: UAHC Press, 2002. Includes resolutions formally adopted by the Central Conference of American Rabbis and the Union for Reform Judaism.

Dorff, Elliot N. *Matters of Life and Death: A Jewish Approach to Modern Medical Ethics.* Philadelphia: Jewish Publication Society, 2004.

Freedman, Benjamin, and Charles Weijer. *Duty and Healing: Foundations of a Jewish Bioethic (Reflective Bioethics).* New York: Routledge, 1999.

In the Winter of Life: A Values-Based Jewish Guide for Decision-Making at the End of Life. Philadelphia: Reconstructionist Rabbinical College, 2002.

Jacob, Walter, and Moshe Zimmer. *Death and Euthanasia in Jewish Law (Studies in Progressive Halakhah).* Pittsburgh: Rodef Shalom Press, 1994.

Kogan, Barry S., ed. *A Time to Be Born and a Time to Die: The Ethics of Choice.* New York: deGruyter Press, 1991.

Sinclair, Daniel B. *Tradition and the Biological Revolution: The Application of Jewish Law and the Treatment of the Critically Ill.* Edinburgh, Scotland: Edinburgh University Press, 1989.

Pamphlets

Gordon, Harvey. *When It Hurts Too Much to Live: Questions and Answers about Jewish Tradition and Issues of Assisted Death.* New York: UAHC Press, 1998. (Available through the URJ Department of Jewish Family Concerns.)

The URJ Department of Jewish Family Concerns has published a thirteen-part set of *Bio-Ethics Study Guides.* Each study guide is a self-contained program featuring thought pieces, Jewish and secular resources, and program ideas on medical technology. Included in the series are pamphlets dealing with pain and suffering, medical decision making, organ donation, cloning, infertility, genetic testing, and living with chronic illness. Contact the Department of Jewish Family Concerns for copies of any of these pamphlets.

Web Sites

www.projectgrace.org: Provides nondenominational guidance for end-of-life care and advance care planning.

www.rwjf.org: Includes position statements from the "Last Acts Coalition" and "Last Acts Partnership" on end-of-life decisions.

5

Seeing Life as a Sacred Journey: Seeking Meaning and Purpose

People become the stories they hear,
and the stories they tell.

Elie Wiesel

Stories reveal a spirituality that views life not as a problem to be solved,
but as a mystery to be lived.

Ernest Kurtz and Katherine Ketcham,
The Spirituality of Imperfection

This chapter will address the following issues:

• Creating spiritual autobiographies
• Writing ethical and spiritual-ethical wills
• Developing intergenerational programs that facilitate relationship building

We Jews are a historical group. Our culture and religion are rooted in history and story-telling. Each week we read the various stories and legends from our *Tanach*, trying to learn lessons on how we can live fulfilling and satisfying lives. We study midrash to learn what our Rabbis can teach us about the lives that they have led and to learn how they were able to derive meaning and purpose from the biblical stories.

We enthusiastically learn from the histories, stories, and wisdom that our ancestors have imparted to us. We can also learn, however, from those histories and stories that our elders have to share with us today. Congregations can tap into the spiritual capital that has been amassed through years of learning and experience. Programs that help congregants develop spiritual autobiographies and ethical wills create a positive experience for everyone involved and the congregation as a whole. By exploring and utilizing the spiritual histories shared by older congregants, a congregation builds its own history, giving it a sense of purpose, sharing, and involvement among all generations.

We treasure the ancient history of Judaism while often ignoring the history through which we have lived. Those in our congregations who have seen the most of our world should have the opportunity not only to share their experiences, but to formally leave us their testimony. There is such a wealth of experience and knowledge among our longest-term members; it is incumbent upon today's synagogue leaders to draw upon that treasure to supplement their own knowledge and efforts. By accessing this resource, they will not only honor and acknowledge those who bear it, but will benefit the entire congregation through this knowledge.

Our ancestors recognized the benefit of an elder's wisdom and insight. Genesis 49:1 says, "Jacob then summoned his sons, saying 'Gather 'round that I may tell you what shall befall you in days to come.'" Jacob's sons listened intently to what their father had to say as he recalled the events of what had occurred to the House of Jacob throughout his lifetime. We, too, can learn from Jacob's example. Our spiritual resources are not just textual, but they are available to us through the experiences that our older congregants can share with us. Like Jacob, we can also learn from the personal, family, and Jewish wisdom that belongs to the older generation.

Spiritual Autobiographies

Each person has a story to tell. Gaining insight and wisdom through the years is a holy, sacred process. Retelling our stories helps us discover God's presence in each of us. "What do you like about being with younger people?" "What is 'old' to you?" "What are your concerns about being old?" "How do you think others perceive you?" "What have you learned as an older adult?" These are some of the questions that congregations may want to use to prompt older congregants to write their "spiritual autobiographies."

A spiritual autobiography is an essay about one's feelings about growing older, or reflections on one's "life's journey." Congregations are finding that allowing older citizens to express their life narratives enables people to realize God's presence. Facilitating the creation of such narratives will help congregants better understand where they have been, what they have learned, and how God has played such an important role in the development of their lives. Moreover, spiritual autobiographies help define one's Jewish identity and Jewish values, while enabling loved ones to share in and learn from those beliefs and values.

Dr. Carol Ochs describes the connection between the narrative experience and God's presence in our lives:

> We develop a theology not by studying God, which we cannot do, but by deriving insights from our own experiences. Indeed, all we can know of God must be based on what we have experienced in our lives. At the same time, we believe that somehow our story is also God's story. Our story *is* God's story, shaped by God's presence in and through our experiences, and God's story is our story. So by examining the components of our lives . . . —committing to love, enduring suffering, undertaking our work, claiming our body, engaging in prayer, living in community, and confronting death—we can find God, and find all we can hope to know or say about God.[1]

---

1. Carol Ochs, *Our Lives as Torah: Finding God in Our Own Stories* (San Francisco: Jossey-Bass, 2001), p. 188.

Memories, whether positive or negative, are vital to a healthy life and, eventually, a healthy death. Only by knowing where you came from, biologically, spiritually, and culturally, can you fill a void and learn to confront the future. A return to the tangible, personal act of storytelling can help heal family relationships and bring elders back into the society of the Jewish family.[2]

Rabbi Helen Cohn of Congregation Emanu-El in San Francisco held a seminar to develop spiritual autobiographies. At the conclusion of the program, she asked some of her congregants to write about their experiences. One congregant wrote, "Each reading of my spiritual autobiography is another step in the journey within. Recently I have begun to think about what I would like others to remember me by when I make my last journey with the angels. Through writing a spiritual autobiography, it has become very clear to me."

In a sermon she delivered after conducting a spiritual autobiography writing program, Rabbi Cohn made these comments:

> Sometimes it is only on reflection long after the event has happened that we can realize the impact it had on our soul's journey. . . . This realization leads [us] to a sense of peace, fulfillment, and reconciliation. All of us have past events that at the time seemed challenging if not disastrous, which now we see touched our soul and guided our life.[3]

In other words, the narrative process of telling our life stories draws out of us an understanding of the experience we have gained throughout the years. Spiritual autobiographies enable us to realize the impact we have had on each other's lives. More importantly, we come to understand how our life events have helped shape who we have become.

Facilitating a program that helps older congregants develop their own spiritual autobiographies benefits not only the younger generations, but the older generation as well. The older congregants will recognize that they can draw on their own personal memories and resources and on those of others in the congregation to deal with life's challenges. In creating a spiritual autobiography program, we invite facilitators to utilize the many text readings throughout this chapter, as well as those found in chapter 1.

Through Torah study, such a program can help frame a person's life experience in spiritual and sacred terms. Armed with a life of experience, older adults want to explore how the depth of our Jewish tradition can add meaning to that experience and inform their future. The richness of our tradition provides the perfect vehicle for encountering God. Spiritual autobiographies allow our older congregants to contribute their gifts born from a life of real world experiences and an evolving relationship with and openness to God.

Congregations might consider a retreat with their older members to create spiritual autobiographies. Caregivers, family members, and the congregation's leadership will learn and understand more about the needs of the aging population. Moreover, the older adults will be given an avenue to express their feelings, share their cares and anxieties, pass on the fruits of their wisdom, and relate their hopes and blessings for the future. The following is a sample of a pilot project on spiritual autobiography conducted by Rabbi Cohn.

---

2. Adapted from Paul White Eagle, "Storytelling," in *Aging and Spirituality: The First Decade*, ed. James Ellor, Stephen Sapp, and Susan McFadden (San Francisco: American Society on Aging, 1997), pp. 62–64.
3. Sermon delivered by Rabbi Helen Cohn on April 30, 2004, Congregation Emanu-El, San Francisco.

Sample Retreat Program

Session I: The Past—Events and Meaning (2 hours)

- Introduction to program and participants.
- Timeline of milestone events (relationships, education, location, professional, and family).
- Texts: The contrast between Joseph and his brothers (Genesis 37–44).
- Assignment (at home): Select one event in your personal past and write about a new meaning you now detect.

Session II: The Present—A Spiritual Journey (2 hours)

- Review Session I and share insights from the week.
- Using same timeline, mark milestone soul events (e.g., challenges, loss, transformation).
- Text: *Elohai n'shamah shenatata bi.*
- At home: journal exercise using these questions:
  1. What have I learned from past experiences?
  2. How have I benefited from times of loss?
  3. How has my life made a difference to others?
  4. What meaning(s) do I detect in my life?

Session III: The Present—Where I Am Now, Who I Am Now (2 hours)

Supplies needed: nametags, handout ("Birth Is a Beginning")

I.   Review
     - Overview of course: began with past, now with present, next with future.
     - Last session:
       - Marked milestone soul events on the timeline (e.g., challenges, loss, transformation, new relationship with God)
       - At home: journal exercise

II. Interpreting the past
     - In small groups of two or three participants, share what you learned from visiting the past.
     - Share with whole group (no "stories," just lessons).

III. Looking at the present: Where am I now? Who am I now?
     - Share reactions to questions about our spiritual past.
     - Text study: "Birth Is a Beginning"[4]

---

4. Birth is a beginning
   And death a destination.
   And life is a journey, a going, a growing
   From stage to stage.
   From childhood to maturity, and youth to age;
   From innocence to awareness, and ignorance to knowing;
   From foolishness to discretion, and then, perhaps to wisdom;

- Write one of the following:
  1. What is the meaning of your life as of now?
  2. What are you here on earth to do, right now (e.g., to gain knowledge, to help other people, to know God)?
  3. If your soul had a name, what would it be (i.e., a one-word description of your essence, such as "compassion," "love," "searching," "sadness," etc)?

IV. Assignment (at home):

Answer the question: "How has God been a part of my life in the past, and how is God in my life now?"

Session IV: The Future—Creation and Legacy (2 1/2 hours)

Supplies needed: nametags, handouts (Rilke poem, Psalm 71, Bible texts)

I. Review of last session
   - Discuss the at-home writing from Session III.

II. Looking toward the future
   - Text: Rilke's "She who reconciles..."(about integration and wholeness with age).[5]
   - Text: Psalm 71 (fears of aging, finding God in new ways as we age).
   - Two ways from Torah to think about our later years and legacy: Jacob (Genesis 47:7–10) and Moses (Deuteronomy 34:5–9).
   - Write and share about spiritual legacies:
     1. For what do I most want to be remembered spiritually?
     2. What is my legacy?
     3. How have I already begun creating my spiritual legacy?
     4. What am I doing and being now that others will remember me by?
     5. What can I do during the rest of my life to make that legacy real?

III. Closure
   - What three words would best describe your soul in this lifetime? (Share with the group, with everyone's eyes closed.)
   - End with "The soul You have given me" prayer[6] (eyes still closed).

From weakness to strength, or strength to weakness, and, often, back again;
From health to sickness, and back, we pray, to health again;
From offense to forgiveness, from loneliness to love, from joy to gratitude,
From pain to compassion, and grief to understanding;
From fear to faith;
From defeat to defeat to defeat, until, looking back or ahead,
We see that victory lies not at some high place along the way,
But in having made the journey, stage by stage, a sacred pilgrimage.
Birth is a beginning, and death a destination.
But life is a journey, a sacred pilgrimage made stage by stage—
From birth to death, to life everlasting.

Rabbi Alvin Fine

5. Rainer Maria Rilke, *Rilke's Book of Hours*, trans. Anita Barrows and Joanna Macy (New York: Riverhead Books, 1997), p. 64.

6. Many translations of *Elohai N'shamah* are available. See, for example, *Mishkon T'filah* (pilot ed.) (New York: Central Conference of American Rabbis, 2004), p. 86.

This is just one example of a program designed to facilitate a spiritual autobiography course. If the participants in the program feel comfortable enough, the facilitator may even want to consider videotaping parts of the program. The congregation could create a video library in order to preserve the historical autobiographies of its congregants; the videotaped oral histories can become a part of the synagogue's own history.

As part of any spiritual autobiography program, the facilitator may want to conduct a survey that is designed to allow the participants to first evaluate their own sense of where they stand spiritually. Before one can begin to think about what to include in a spiritual autobiography, the biographers must first determine their own personal "level" of spirituality. This may not be so easy to do. Facilitators need to recognize that not every person, young or old, thinks about where they are spiritually on a routine basis. Many of us do not think about religion that seriously at all, nor do we give ourselves a self-evaluation on topics such as religious observance, God, and worship.

Any program designed to help congregants create spiritual autobiographies, therefore, should include adequate time for the participants to think about these issues of spirituality. Included below are two self-assessment surveys that may be used for this purpose. The goal of a self-assessment survey is to help the autobiographers think about where they stand on a spiritual level. This, in turn, will hopefully trigger them to think more clearly about what they would like to include in their spiritual autobiographies.

Spiritual Assessment Surveys

Spiritual Assessment Survey A[7]

Frequency, Types, and Helpfulness of Spiritual Activities

1. How often do you attend a place for spiritual practice, such as a synagogue or other such ceremonial site? Please describe these places.

    Daily?   Weekly?   Monthly?   Yearly?   Very Rarely?   Never?

2. What kinds of spiritual activities do you perform together with a spiritual group? These might include forms of prayer, meditation, ritual, ceremony, reading sacred texts, telling and listening to inspirational stories or speeches, or participating in social support groups. Please describe them.

3. In what ways do you find these activities helpful or unhelpful?

4. How often do you perform spiritual activities together with your family?

    Daily?   Weekly?   Monthly?   Yearly?   Very Rarely?   Never?

5. What kinds of special activities do you perform together with your family at home? Please describe them.

---

7. From Jacki Dwoskin, Ph.D., Temple Israel, West Palm Beach, Florida, and her work developing programs on spirituality and aging for Nova University.

6. In what ways do you find these activities helpful or unhelpful?

7. How often do you perform spiritual activities by yourself?

   Daily?   Weekly?   Monthly?   Yearly?   Very Rarely?   Never?

8. What kinds of spiritual activities do you perform by yourself? Please describe them.

9. In what ways do you find these activities helpful or unhelpful?

Inspirational Sources of Support

1. Who have been your most important spiritual friends and mentors? Please describe them.

2. What are the most significant stories, teachings, or symbols that give you guidance? Please describe them.

3. What have been the most profound and moving experiences that gave you a sense of peace, wisdom, or grace? Please describe them.

4. When you have been at a time of crisis previously, what spiritual supports helped you most? Please describe them.

5. When you have been at a great time of satisfaction and joy, what spiritual supports contributed most? Please describe them.

Extrinsic/Intrinsic Styles of Spiritual Propensity

1. How often do you agree with the teachings and values of your spiritual groups?

   Never?   Rarely?   Sometimes?   Usually?   Always?

   Please explain and give examples.

2. How comfortable are you with the activities and style of your spiritual groups?

   Not at all?   Not much?   Somewhat?   Very much?   Completely?

   Please explain and give examples.

3. If you ever disagree or are uncomfortable with any aspect of your spiritual groups, how often do you tell people?

Never?   Rarely?   Sometimes?   Usually?   Always?

Please explain and give examples.

4. How much are your spiritual principles and practices integrated into your daily life outside of spiritual group participation?

Not at all?   Very little?   Somewhat?   Very much?   Completely?

Please explain and give answers.

5. When you meet someone from a different spiritual perspective from your own, how often do you feel that you should help that person to change his or her perspective?

Never?   Rarely?   Somewhat?   Usually?   Always?

Please explain and give examples.

Spiritual Assessment Survey B[8]

1. I feel God's presence:
   1 – Many times a day
   2 – Every day
   3 – Most days
   4 – Some days
   5 – Once in a while
   6 – Never or almost never
2. I experience a connection to all of life:
   1 – Many times a day
   2 – Every day
   3 – Most days
   4 – Some days
   5 – Once in a while
   6 – Never or almost never
3. During worship, or at other times when connecting to God, I feel joy that lifts me out of my daily concerns:
   1 – Many times a day
   2 – Every day
   3 – Most days

8. Ibid.

      4 – Some days

      5 – Once in a while

      6 – Never or almost never

4. I find strength in my religion or spirituality:

      1 – Many times a day

      2 – Every day

      3 – Most days

      4 – Some days

      5 – Once in a while

      6 – Never or almost never

5. I find comfort in my religion or spirituality:

      1 – Many times a day

      2 – Every day

      3 – Most days

      4 – Some days

      5 – Once in a while

      6 – Never or almost never

6. I feel deep inner peace and harmony:

      1 – Many times a day

      2 – Every day

      3 – Most days

      4 – Some days

      5 – Once in a while

      6 – Never or almost never

7. I ask for God's help in the midst of daily activities:

      1 – Many times a day

      2 – Every day

      3 – Most days

      4 – Some days

      5 – Once in a while

      6 – Never or almost never

8. I feel guided by God in the midst of daily activities:

      1 – Many times a day

      2 – Every day

      3 – Most days

      4 – Some days

      5 – Once in a while

      6 – Never or almost never

9. I feel God's love for me, directly:

      1 – Many times a day

      2 – Every day

      3 – Most days

      4 – Some days

      5 – Once in a while

      6 – Never or almost never

10. I feel God's love for me, through others:

      1 – Many times a day

2 - Every day

3 - Most days

4 - Some days

5 - Once in a while

6 - Never or almost never

11. I am spiritually touched by the beauty of creation:

1 - Many times a day

2 - Every day

3 - Most days

4 - Some days

5 - Once in a while

6 - Never or almost never

12. I feel thankful for my blessings:

1 - Many times a day

2 - Every day

3 - Most days

4 - Some days

5 - Once in a while

6 - Never or almost never

13. I feel a selfless caring for others:

1 - Many times a day

2 - Every day

3 - Most days

4 - Some days

5 - Once in a while

6 - Never or almost never

14. I desire to be closer to God or in union with God:

1 - Many times a day

2 - Every day

3 - Most days

4 - Some days

5 - Once in a while

6 - Never or almost never

15. In general, how close do you feel to God?

1 - Not at all close

2 – Somewhat close

3 – Very close

4 – As close as possible

Ethical Wills and Spiritual-Ethical Wills

> Oh, that my words were written down,
> Incised on a rock forever.
>
> Job 19:23–4

Although many people have heard of ethical wills, it is important to clarify that an ethical will is not a legal document such as one's last will and testament or "living will" (advance health care directive). Often an ethical will is a carefully created letter to be shared with loved ones. Each will be unique; some may be a simple page of instructions and blessings for future generations; others may include family memories, life lessons, personal reflections, and significant life events. Their purpose is to preserve values, ideas, memories, life lessons, personal reflections, or significant events for one's family and friends.[9]

The prototype for this document can be found in Genesis 49, when a dying Jacob gathers his twelve sons, gives them his instructions and blessings, and obtains their promise not to leave his bones in Egypt, but instead to bury him in Canaan with his ancestors. Both components—blessing future generations, and making death, burial, and funeral requests—should be introduced for inclusion in the modern spiritual-ethical will.

In conducting any spiritual autobiography or ethical will seminar, facilitators should consider the following possible topics for discussion:

- My happiest times/my saddest times
- Expressions of love and gratitude
- Lessons I have learned from my life experience
- Successes and regrets in my life
- How spirituality has been a part of my life
- Episodes in my life where I learned something
- My ancestral background and family stories
- Influential people in my life
- Familial obligations
- Favorite Torah or Rabbinic passages
- Things that I have done that I regret
- Hopes and blessings for future generations
- Funeral and burial preferences

It is vital that the facilitator frame these questions in a Jewish context, perhaps by utilizing a piece of Jewish text. Our own biblical stories can show a participant how important memorializing our thoughts, stories, and wishes can be.

It is acceptable in our Jewish tradition to deliver an ethical will during one's lifetime and not wait until after death. Here are a few modern examples of ethical wills:

To My Treasured Children,
More than material things already gifted, and beyond that which is bequeathed in my last will and testament, I hope I have given you a love of your faith, a trust in God, and a devotion to family, fairness, and peace. These are among the precious jewels that will enrich your life with vitality and wonder.
I hope you will enjoy good health, good humor, and well-being.
I hope you will use yourself with passion and compassion.
I wish you a life lived with love, courage, and fantasy. Explore, dream, and discover!
Your loving mom[10]

---

9. "Ethical Wills: A Legacy of Values," *Tikvah Times*, Summer 2004, p. 103.
10. Jeanne Bearmon's letter to accompany individual picture albums she created for each of her children, in Rachael Freed, *Women's Lives, Women's Legacies* (Minneapolis: Fairview Press, 2003) p. 234.

To my Grandchildren and Children Everywhere:

I leave you my unpaid debts. They are my greatest assets. Everything I own—I owe:

To America I owe a debt for the opportunity it gave me to be free and to be me.

To my parents I owe America. They gave it to me and I leave it to you. Take good care of it.

To the biblical tradition I owe the belief that man does not live by bread alone, nor does he live alone at all. This is also the democratic tradition. Preserve it.

To the six million of my people and to the thirty million other humans who died because of a man's inhumanity to man, I owe a vow that it must never happen again.

I leave you not everything I never had, but everything I had in my lifetime: a good family, respect for learning, compassion for my fellow man, and some four-letter words for all occasions, words like: help, give, care, feel, and love.

Finally, I leave you the years I should like to have lived so that I might possibly see whether *your* generation will bring more love and peace to the world than ours did. I not only hope that you will. I pray that you will.

Grandpa Sam Levenson[11]

Dear Anna, Peter and Eddie,

I am a quiet man, and I know that I have never offered much in the way of spiritual guidance. . . . I hope that my manner of living has served as a living example of my own moral code. As you know, this family has had its roots here . . . since our great-grandpa Jack settled it way back in 1867. I certainly don't expect you to keep the farm; I realize that even little Eddie will follow his big brother and sister to the city. My only request is that the house and the 15 surrounding acres be preserved as a family vacation spot. I want you to bring your children to relax, fish, swim, and have fun pursuing life's simple things, but most importantly, to stick together as a family. I love you all.

Dad[12]

The Intergenerational Approach

How to Treasure an Old Person

Seek out old people. When you find some, give them joy. Listen closely. Develop your patience. Tune up your sensitive humor. Crack your shell. Remember that each old person is a library. Listen closely. Go for a slow walk in a sunny park. Be useful. Bring the gift of your self. Try enchantment. Be voluntary. Visit with magic. Invent a new activity. Try playing their game. Let wisdom seep in. Cradle your own future old person. Hug willingly. Sew on a button. Handwrite a letter. Take a midnight cruise in a convertible. Try respect. Bestow surprise gifts. Handle with caring. Be gentle. Make a nourishing soup. Believe in really living. Pray together. Gamble on love. Plant a tree.

---

11. Jack Riemer and Nathaniel Stempfer, *So That Your Values Live On: Ethical Wills and How to Prepare Them* (Woodstock, VT: Jewish Lights Publishing, 1994), p. 168.
12. "Ethical Wills: A Legacy of Values," p. 103.

Plan something outrageous. Embrace death. Hold hands at twilight. Bake funny cook-
ies. Listen closely. Pay attention to an old person.[13]

Our life experiences are important not just for ourselves, but for others as well. Leaving
an ethical will is important because it can impart our wishes and desires after we have died.
It is equally important, however, to try to leave that same legacy to the younger generation
while we are still living. We have so much in our lives that we can impart to others, including wisdom we have gained on such themes as doing mitzvot, leading a rewarding and fulfilling lifestyle, and views on death. Our hope, ultimately, is that others will be able to learn
and benefit from what we have learned throughout life's various stages.

A cultural shift needs to take place in our lives today wherein the younger generation is
taught to appreciate the wisdom possessed by the older generation. Part of the sacred journey
should include giving our older congregants the opportunity to teach the younger congregants this lesson. Sharing what they have learned from experiencing moments of fear and contentment, happiness and sorrow, and spirituality and emptiness is a holy, sacred exercise.

Debra Smith, an adult Jewish educator with the Lester Senior Housing Group in
Whippany, New Jersey, facilitated a program with a group of older citizens designed to
explore what lessons the group would like to share with the younger people in their lives.
The group expressed a passionate desire to express to others what their life journeys have
taught them. For instance, the focus groups wanted to pass on the message that old age is
only a state of mind and an attitude, and that some people never grow old. Growing older
should be accepted as a positive attribute, and members of the younger generation should
be grateful for the wisdom that they will acquire throughout their years. Moreover, the
group felt that it was important to teach the younger generation how to accept turmoil,
including family conflict, that inevitably exists in everyone's life.

Torah teaches us about the wisdom that can be gained by learning from the lessons that
our elders have taught us. After Moses died, we are told that Joshua was "filled with the spirit of wisdom" because Moses had laid his hands upon Joshua (Deuteronomy 34:9). Joshua
went on to become a great leader of the Israelite people. Our tradition teaches us that
Joshua had the capacity to learn from Moses, to observe his greatness and his shortcomings,
and to appreciate the way in which Moses taught, led, and became close to God.

Like Moses, each of us in our older years has a wealth of wisdom and experience that we can
pass on to others while we are still alive. To tap into the reservoir of spiritual capital, a congregation may want to consider developing a "matchmaking" system, in which younger adults are
"buddied" with older adults to help each other and to discuss the meaning of aging and the
lessons that life has taught them so far. Wisdom and experience can be expressed to our own
grandchildren in the same way Moses passed on his wisdom to Joshua.

The interaction between the young and old in a matchmaking program will prove beneficial to both generations. The older participants will be given an opportunity to more fully
elaborate on their experiences, expressing their sorrows and fears, their moments of joy and
happiness, and their blessings for those who are going to follow in their footsteps. The
younger participants will have the time to probe their older partners, asking pointed questions about their experiences and what they learned from those events. Here is an example
of an essay written by a younger person who was involved in a congregation's matchmaking
program:

---

13. From Sark, *A Creative Companion* (Berkeley, CA: Celestial Arts, 1991).

What appeals to you about being with an older person?

"It gives me more experience in life. They have a lot to say. I can appreciate life more, and have more fun. A lot of young people don't care about world matters, whereas older people do. So, they can help us by teaching us about history and its lessons. Also, older adults are more comfortable to talk to, and can advise you on making better life choices. They have good stories, and they are fun-loving."

Anonymous

The following are some other comments from teenagers who successfully participated in a matchmaking program with older congregants in their local synagogue:

"I believe that we have all learned that we are not in reality two generations separated by an impenetrable barrier, but one group of living breathing humans: humans who have learned so much from each other and will continue to learn from each other."

"We learned from people who had seen so much more. We came to love our adopted grandparents. If this program was offered to other students, I feel the quality of life would improve worldwide. When children talk to their elders, both learn."

"We, the youth, must learn the hope and strength of our elders, their foresight, and the resilience to rebuild a shattered world when so much had been lost. We must learn their acceptance and versatility, putting aside petty differences for the greater good. We must learn to laugh like them, to sing with them and to learn that fighting and hate can destroy so much, and peace and love can rebuild it all."

"It is a shame that in the fast-paced world we live in, nobody slows down long enough to listen to those who could teach us a few shortcuts or even to lead us to new adventures. On my journey through the program, I ended up finding myself. I found the me that I would like to be. When I am seventy-something years old, I want to know that I made a difference. So that if a young person ever takes time to slow down for me, I'll have something to share with them."

Many congregations have developed programs for matching older congregants with their younger counterparts. Instead of randomly matching a couple, consider having each participant answer a series of questions, and then make a match based upon the answers.

The following are a few examples of probing questions:

1. What have I learned from past accomplishments and experiences?
2. How have I benefited from experiences of disappointment, injustice, or loss?
3. How has my life made a difference to others?
4. What meanings do I detect in life?

Such open-ended questions are designed to elicit many different types of responses from the participants. The leader may want to make matches based on differences in the participants' responses. For instance, in response to the last question listed above, if a child says that she does not detect great meaning in her life, then it would be appropriate to match her with an older person who elaborated at some length on this particular question. The child would be able to learn a great deal from the stories related to her by the older person.

The following is a sample of a program that was developed by Rabbi Maurice Salth to connect the youth at a congregation with its older citizens. The program is designed to introduce the younger generation to the values of their older counterparts.

Sample Matchmaking Program:
From Generation to Generation—L'Dor VaDor

Purpose: The goal of this program is to build relationships between the youngest and oldest members of the congregation. A synagogue's greatest resource is its people. This program is designed to connect two subsets of a synagogue community that rarely interact. During the program we will study sacred texts, explore our temple's history, and develop rituals.

Program One: Introduction and Text Study

Preparation: Participants are to bring pictures or mementos from home that represent a spiritual connection to their Judaism.

Circle of Life Exercise: The facilitator will ask all youth group members to form a circle shoulder to shoulder. Members will be asked to face the walls of the room. The facilitator will then ask the seniors to form a circle shoulder to shoulder facing one of the youth members. The result is that a senior and a youth will be paired together, with youths on the inside, and seniors on the outside.

The facilitator will then ask the participants to answer six questions for three minutes each. After each question, the inside circle will rotate to the right, resulting in new pairs of seniors and youths. The six questions are:

1. What do you remember about where you were born?
2. What was it like for you to be in school?
3. What is your favorite hobby?
4. What is your favorite Jewish holiday?
5. How long have you been connected to the temple?
6. What is your favorite Jewish food?

Photo/Object Sharing Exercise: In groups of three youths and three seniors, participants will share what they brought. Encourage the participants to ask each other thoughtful questions about their objects and photos.

Text Study: In the same groups of six, participants will study texts from Ecclesiastes 1:1–10 and 3:1–8. Ask the groups to address the following: What sections did or did not resonate? Do either of the readings remind you of what is happening in your life currently? Have any of the events in the readings happened to you before?

Program Two: Back to the Future

Preparation: Participants will be asked to bring pictures or objects symbolic of their connection to the temple.

"History of the Temple" Activity: Participants reconvene in their original groups of six. They should share any important events that have occurred since their last meeting and thoughts that they have about the first meeting. With the help of one of the seniors, each youth will spend about three minutes explaining what the senior remembers about the early years of the temple, using pictures, overheads, and so on.

"A Plan for the Future" Activity: The seniors and youth will have the choice of selecting one of two activities, as follows.

Activity A: New Ritual Creation

This group will be charged with designing a new ritual that honors our temple's rich history while inspiring its bright future. Congregants will integrate this ritual into their life-cycle events at the temple.

Activity B: A Vision for the Future

This group will be charged with visioning for the temple for the next fifty years. The participants will be asked to reflect upon the temple's current mission and vision statements and amend them to meet what they perceive will be the needs of the congregations in future years. They should describe key programs and activities necessary for the temple to meets its new mission.

Program Three: Shabbat L'Dor VaDor

Preparation: Participants will be asked to participate in the Torah service and lead *Kiddush* and *Motzi* at Shabbat services.

Shabbat Service: The rabbi and cantor will recognize the participation of the *L'Dor VaDor* members and their families. Music is selected to represent the youths and the older congregants. Pairs of seniors and youths will be called for *aliyot*, read from Torah, lead services, and so on. The service should also include the ritual that was created in the second program.

Program Four: From Wisdom to Wisdom

Preparation: Participants will be asked to bring readings that they find meaningful to share with others. They will also be asked to think of other activities for their groups.

"Wisdom Sharing" Activity: Participants reconvene in their original groups of six. Each group will read and review the following text pieces: the Ten Commandments; Joel 3:1; "Birth Is a Beginning," by Rabbi Alvin Fine; other texts brought by the participants.

"Group Journaling" Activity: All six will sit in a circle and be given sheets of paper. Each will then choose a quote from a reading or text that is meaningful for him or her, and write for five minutes about that piece. They will then pass the text and their paper to

the person to their left, and the exercise will begin again. After six rounds, each participant will have his or her comments on the piece written on each piece of paper.

"Wall of Wisdom" Activity: Place large flip chart pages around the room. All participants will be encouraged to go to the walls and share their advice, wisdom, and ideas on living life, being a member of the temple, problems they face, and so on. Collect the papers and then send them to the participants in a booklet form.

The following additional intergenerational programming ideas were collected from various congregations:

1. Religious school students or younger adult members can conduct their own oral histories and compare them to the oral histories that were created by the older congregants. By comparing the two sets of oral histories, the students can learn to appreciate the value of not just understanding the past, but valuing the present and the future as well.
2. With the help of school librarians, elders can select books to read to younger children in the religious school. Stories should be selected that present a positive and realistic picture of older people and reduce existing discrimination and existing stereotypes about older people.
3. Develop a mentoring program in which young professionals are partnered with older congregants in the same field. Use the life skills of the older adults to work with members of your congregation who may be beginning their careers and would benefit from learning from others who "have done it."

Our tradition teaches us the power of telling our life histories to the younger generation. Jacob and Moses, two of our most revered forefathers, understood how beneficial their wisdom could be to the Children of Israel. By preserving this tradition of narrating our blessings, our sorrows, and our joys to each other, we are following in their footsteps. Each of us has a story to tell, and we grow spiritually when we are afforded the opportunity to share our stories. Not only do we impart our wisdom to others, we develop a greater sense of our own place in the world of God's creation.

A growing, exciting spiritual revolution is now under way within the older adult population of the Jewish community. Gradually, our synagogues and communal organizations are realizing the tremendous potential for life-affirming role models that now exist within this and the coming generations of older adults. The elders among us are alive and eager to contribute their gifts born from a life of real-world experience and an evolving relationship with and openness to God. This is a generation that still dreams, and yearns to share those dreams with the loved ones that surround them.

Too many of our congregations choose to ignore the valuable life experiences of the growing older adult community. Factor in the experiences and extended work and life spans of the baby boom generation and we see that a congregation that chooses to ignore this "capital" does so at its own peril. We encourage congregations to tap into this valuable human resource:

1. Create mentoring programs that link the generations and help create sacred relationships within the congregation.
2. Create audio or video history programs that give testimony to the life experiences of our older members.

3. Allow those stories to be told in classrooms and from the pulpit; celebrate the lives of our own people so that their experiences can model behavior for the next generations.

God of the beginning, God of the end, with love You guide the world, and with love You walk hand in hand with all of us. May our reflections help us to bring into our lives the harmony we seek, and the love we share. Amen.

Additional Resources

Books

Baines, Barry. *Ethical Wills: Putting Your Values on Paper*. Cambridge, MA: Perseus, 2001.

Birren, James E., and Kathryn N. Cochran. *Telling the Stories of Life Through Guided Autobiography Groups*. Baltimore: John Hopkins University Press, 2001.

Bressler, Jeanette, and Nancy Z. Henkin. *Connecting Generations, Strengthening Communities: A Toolkit for Intergenerational Programming*. Philadelphia: Temple University Press, 2005.

Freed, Rachael. *Women's Lives, Women's Legacies: Passing Your Beliefs and Blessings to Future Generations, Creating Your Own Spiritual-Ethical Will*. Minneapolis: Fairview Press, 2003.

Kenyon, Gary M., and William L. Randall. *Restorying Our Own Lives: Personal Growth through Autobiographical Reflection*. Westport, CT: Greenwood, 1997.

Riemer, Jack. *Ethical Wills: Modern Jewish Treasury*. Edited by Nathaniel Stampfer. New York: Knopf, 1986.

Riemer, Jack, and Nathaniel Stampfer. *So That Your Values Live On: Ethical Wills and How to Prepare Them*. Woodstock, VT: Jewish Lights Publishing, 1994.

Sherman, Edmund. *The Autobiographical Consciousness of Aging*. Self-published, 2000.

Wakefield, Dan. *The Story of Your Life: Writing a Spiritual Autobiography*. Boston: Beacon Press, 1990.

Web Sites

www.womenslegacies.com. The Women's Legacy Project offers information on creating an ethical will.

www.ethicalwill.com: For details on creating an ethical will.

www.spiritualeldering.org: The Spiritual Eldering Institute is a multifaith organization dedicated to the spiritual dimension of aging.

www.reminiscenceandlifereview.org: The International Institute for Reminiscence and Life Review develops reminiscence and life review strategies as an interdisciplinary field of study.

6

Programming Opportunities

> You shall rise before the aged
> and show deference to the old.
>
> Leviticus 19:32

This chapter will address the following needs:

- Identifying and responding to the spiritual needs of today's older adults
- Implementing new and meaningful programming opportunities

Developing programs for the elderly population involves a renewed understanding of what it means to "grow old." Abraham Joshua Heschel once wrote:

> We must seek ways to overcome the traumatic fear of being old, prejudice, discrimination against those advanced in years. All men are created equal, including those advanced in years. Being old is not necessarily the same as being stale.[1]

The effort to restore the dignity of old age will depend on our ability to revive the equation of old age and wisdom. Wisdom is the substance upon which inner security of the old will forever depend. But the attainment of wisdom is the work of a lifetime. Rethinking the way we view the aging population is paramount to creating invigorating and meaningful programs. Congregations must tear down age-based stereotypes and elevate attitudes that honor each person as an individual, no matter what his or her age may be.

Programmatic responses to the longevity revolution, therefore, must reflect and promote the belief systems of the aging population. Positive values and ethics are central to revitalizing a programming system that includes the aging population. This process starts with seeing older adults as a creative force within our communities. They are capable of teaching and leading their congregations as a result of their wisdom and life experiences. Many are in good health and understand the link between physical and spiritual wellness.

---

1. Abraham Joshua Heschel, *The Insecurity of Freedom*, p. 84.

Congregational leaders must appreciate how the elderly view themselves and the way they want to continue to live their lives in a meaningful manner.

Infusing purpose and spiritual meaning into any program is the key to creating sacred relationships. To be successful, programming ideas must take into account the sanctity of the relationships that are being built between the participants, the lay leadership, and the clergy alike.

Meaningful Programming Suggestions

The following programming ideas were collected from congregations and other Jewish organizations around the country.

Personal Growth and Health

An increasing awareness and programmatic focus of congregations recently has been in the area of wellness. Education about healthy living and programs that provide a means to remain active—both physically and mentally—can only serve to enrich and enhance the lives of older adults.

1. Develop programs and support groups that focus on wellness and healthy aging. Focus on issues of living well and health, such as an exercise group for seniors. Consider sponsoring a "Health Fair" cosponsored with a local health care facility that would provide screenings and educational programs with seminars on how Judaism looks at health and aging.
2. Develop programs that explore issues of older adult sexuality, intimacy, living arrangements, and new family situations. Include programs that address interfaith relationships, grandparenting with children from interfaith marriages, and gay and lesbian partnership aging.
3. Create workshops and educational opportunities that highlight such issues as the arts, music, dance, literature, and film. Use Jewish themes, rituals, and ceremonial pieces as ideas for such workshops. There are many Jewish professional artists and teachers (many in your congregation) who can instruct and lead the workshops so that Jewish themes and lessons are utilized.
4. Offer classes that include Jewish meditative practices. These speak to a new openness on the part of the growing older adult cohorts to seek renewed personal expression of spirituality in search of meaning and purpose.
5. Help develop training programs for congregational ombudspersons who can assist families in negotiating issues of support for older adult family members. Working with caring community committee and clergy, these people would assist in resource and referral for insurance issues, placement issues, and bill paying services for seniors either at the synagogue or at their homes. They could likewise help in developing at-home shopping, driving, and transportation assistance.

Experience and Learning

Throughout this book, we have stressed the idea that the elderly are anything but stagnant. The experiences that they have gained can be used to teach us all. At the same time, their active minds and bodies demand that congregations continue to develop meaningful learning and educational programs.

1. Conduct a congregational search for people who have made significant discoveries, contributions to society, or major life changes in their later years. Once those congregants have been identified, have a series of lunches that honor them, giving them a forum to discuss their life experiences, what they learned, and how these experiences helped them to grow.
2. Create a "Storytelling and Reminiscence Group." Choose a theme, such as grandparenting, family holiday remembrances, or significant life-altering events, and allow the members to share the stories and lessons that they learned.
3. Plan intellectual and educational programs for older adults, such as Torah study, bar and bat mitzvah classes, Yiddish language instruction, and drama productions. Involve older adults by asking for their input and suggestions and allowing them to plan and implement these learning programs.
4. Conduct an "Immigrant Legacy" program. Many of our relatives who were first generation immigrants have already died, so that the elders in our community are mostly second- or even third-generation Americans. Use video to record the stories that have been passed down through the generations, and make them available in the congregation's library.
5. Many seniors in a community have been living in that particular community for a long time, sometimes for their entire lives. The knowledge they have gained about specific landmarks can be an educational learning experience for the entire community. Organize field trips, guided by congregants who personally know of the history of those landmarks, for members of the congregation of all ages.
6. Explore the development of continuing educational opportunities through the use of computer learning. Create your own congregation-based distance learning classes using clergy and congregational resources to allow individuals who are homebound or living in nursing home or assisted-living facilities to be part of the congregation's educational program.

Congregational Involvement

These suggestions[2] are offered to help congregations both make maximum use of their resources and to give dignity and respect to their longest-term members. Many older members have served congregations well in the past, either as officers, members of the board, committee members, or regular worship attendees. They have demonstrated that they care deeply about the congregation, and many of them are probably anxious to serve the congregation still, in many ways, if properly engaged.

1. Reevaluate the roles that aging congregants play in the life of the congregation, and determine where they may be able to provide assistance and experience. Schedule time with committee chairs and other congregational leaders to explore options in existing programs to see if they can be revitalized by the ideas and support of aging congregants.

---

2. By David Napell and Larry Simon, members of the URJ Department of Jewish Family Concerns' Sacred Aging committee.

2. Program teaching opportunities with the adult education chair. Explore options such as inviting seniors to lead Torah study courses, book-of-the-month meetings, or other such adult learning opportunities.

3. Program special holiday services for the elderly. Involve elderly congregants and their caregivers in Passover seders, Purim services, meals in the sukkah, or menorah lighting ceremonies on Chanukah.

4. Reconsider bringing many elderly congregants who may have been more involved in congregational life back into leadership positions.

5. Create an advisory council to the congregational board, taking advantage of the knowledge and experience gained by the aging congregants throughout their years of involvement in the congregation. The council would not have the power to override the board, but rather to help the board make decisions through discussion and the lens of experiences, both inside and outside of the synagogue. Assign a temple officer to meet with the council, and allow a member of the council to sit on the board.

6. Conduct week-long programs that educate congregants on various worship rituals, such as leading a shivah service, or acting as *gabbai* at a Torah service. Classical Reform Judaism, for many older congregants, meant that only clergy were involved in these activities, so laypeople never had an opportunity to get actively involved. Guiding them to become worship leaders themselves allows congregants to feel reconnected to their Judaism.

7. Form a garden club at the synagogue. Get congregants involved in planning and maintaining the synagogue facility. For example, invite congregants to make seasonal landscaping changes on the synagogue grounds, and invite them to do the actual weeding and planting.

8. Consider developing the position of congregation-based health care worker/nurse, whose job would be to educate the congregation on matters of Judaism and health and, when possible, do home visits to older adults.

9. Depending on the congregation's demographics and finances, consider creating a full- or part-time director of older adult programming.

Housing Options

> Behold, how good and pleasant it is
> for brothers to dwell in unity!
>
> Psalm 133:1

For the older population, housing has several functions. It is a source of shelter, an environment that can help mitigate difficulties in negotiating the activities of daily living, and a venue for major family relationships. Housing is an instrument for psychological and social well-being.[3]

Many elderly Jews are not living in Jewish-sponsored institutions. However, a Jewish living atmosphere can provide an added sense of spirituality and security. Whether lighting Shabbat candles, eating a meal in a sukkah, or attending worship services, Jews respond to such rituals more energetically and with greater spirituality when they are performed as a

---

3. "The Consequences of Population Aging for Society," report, The International Longevity Center, USA, Ltd., 2000, pp. 6–8.

community. The programming ideas in this chapter are intended to renew positive value thinking in the way we view older adults. Living together in a community of Jews is perhaps the ultimate way for older adults to experience such positive thinking.

Models of Jewish Housing

Three different models of Jewish housing with which congregations may become involved are presented below. Essential for each model to succeed is the active participation of the synagogue. Congregations must become energetic in developing and maintaining an economically and spiritually viable Jewish housing option.

Assisted-living/Nursing Facilities with a Small Jewish Presence

Most older citizens live in some form of assisted-living facility that is not affiliated with any particular Jewish organization.

Congregational challenges include transportation to and from the facility, providing pastoral counseling, involving congregants in worship services and ritual practices, and dues obligations.

Assisted-living/Nursing Facilities with a Large Jewish Presence

A large Jewish presence in a nursing or assisted-living facility alleviates some of the pressures of catering to the needs of the aging population. The group could be large enough so that it could form a "congregation" of its own.

Congregational challenges include staffing, developing programs at the facility, overhead expenses, and spiritual leadership.

Senior Housing Community

Larger Jewish communities are exploring the option of creating a synagogue-sponsored Jewish housing community. For the most part, the members of such a community are very active within their synagogue and are economically viable. Resources probably would not be spent on developing youth programs, but instead might be directed toward developing grandparenting programs.

Congregational challenges include hiring professional, full-time clergy, paying dues to the Union for Reform Judaism, community fees and community governance, and the level of support from the sponsoring congregation or other Jewish institution.

Possibilities for Developing New Forms of Congregations within Evolving Options in Housing

An exciting area of programming is now emerging within the rapidly growing numbers of life-care, assisted-living, and healthy active older adult communities. We are seeing the development of new congregation forms within these institutions. Some have been fostered by neighboring congregations. Some have begun to evolve on their own, out of the desire of residents to maintain a Jewish community and contacts. Will these developing forms become new categories of congregations for our consideration? It appears that this may be on the near horizon. Again, the revolution in longevity and the desire for meaningful Jewish contexts will drive innovation.

For several years, Eileen Rodgers and Colin Alter of Beth Ami in Rockville, Maryland, have been working at Riderwood Village, Bedford Court, and Brighton Gardens. Within these facilities, Rodgers and Alter have helped create new "congregations" that speak to and support the residents of these communities. The development of this project has also allowed for the creation of intercongregational cooperation, as several congregations have contributed material and support for these communities. Among the many benefits of this program, supported by their congregations, are the following:

- Assists in sensitizing the pastoral providers of these facilities to the need, concerns, and experiences of the Jewish population.
- Helps build community with the volunteers who assist in these programs by creating life-affirming views of older adults and allowing the volunteers to interact and thus enhance the power of relationships.
- Supports the Jewish residents by reminding them that they remain part of a community of caring.
- Allows and assists in the celebration of festivals, especially when children and other relatives are able to visit.

Educational Programs and Seminars

We invite congregational leaders to plan programming and educational seminars that speak to the issues and challenges associated with the longevity revolution. We have learned in the development of the Sacred Aging project that one of the major desires of the "new" Jewish older adult is to be involved in serious study. These are generations of college-educated, affluent, and well-experienced individuals who wish to see their experiences in light of their tradition. There is no need to "dumb down" programming. In fact, the elementary and pediatric level of some programming is one of the reasons many of our members over sixty years old have given for leaving our congregations.

The success of "elder hostel" type programs that have been created by URJ regions and congregations in recent years have proved the validity of developing quality educational programs that reflect the lifestyles and concerns of our longevity generations. Congregations and regions have developed half-day, full-day, *Shabbaton*, and full-weekend programs. Likewise, congregations and URJ regions have developed three-day midweek programs that use URJ camps as "campuses," thus allowing for additional forms of creative programming and interaction. The URJ Department of Jewish Family Concerns can be helpful in developing these programs if you so desire.

The following is a sample outline of a full-weekend program held at Congregation Temple Sinai of New Orleans, Louisiana.[4] The purpose of the retreat was to give the congregants the opportunity to explore how and why they want to address the needs of the aging population within their community. The participants were able to identify the cultural and religious needs of the older population, so that programming ideas could emerge that supported those needs.

---

4. For additional suggestions on how to schedule a weekend retreat to educate congregants on the needs of their older adults, contact the URJ Department of Jewish Family Concerns.

The Art of Aging

Friday Schedule

8:15 p.m.   Shabbat Service
Keynote I—Emerging Medical Technology: Using Jewish Values to Make Informed Choices
Oneg following *T'filah*

Shabbat Schedule

9:00 a.m.   Torah Study Sessions
Primary focus of texts will be on the spiritual dynamics of growing old.

10:15 a.m.   Shabbat Morning Service
Keynote II—Creating a Comprehensive Caring Community: If Not Us, Who? If Not Now, When?

12:00 p.m.   Kiddush, Luncheon

1:45 p.m.   Laboratory Experiment in the Search for Ritual:
How Can We Help the Elderly Develop Meaningful Prayers, Blessings, and Jewish Rituals?

3:00 p.m.   Workshop Session I
(select one)
a. Pulling It All Together—What's It All About?
A review of Erikson's Eight Stages of Development
b. Aging and Your Sexuality
c. Jewish Values and Personal Health
d. Personal Stories as Models of Jewish Living

4:30 p.m.   Address
Keynote III—Creating Meaningful and Purposeful Programming Alternatives

5:15 p.m.   *Havdalah*

Sunday Schedule

9:15 a.m.   Morning *T'filah*

9:30 a.m.   Symposium Overview
Continental Breakfast

10:00 a.m.   Workshop Session II
(select one)
a. What Do We Mean by "Healthy Aging"?
A Multidisciplinary Discussion
b. The Search for Meaning and Purpose in the Third Stage of Life: *A Text-based Workshop and Discussion*
c. My Point of You: *An Intergenerational Dialogue between Confirmands and Seventies-plus!*
d. Writing an Ethical Will: *Why It Has Been a Jewish Tradition*

11:30–12:00 p.m. Meditative Service

Jewish Gay, Lesbian, Bisexual, and Transgender Seniors

by John E. Hirsch, Ph.D.

Seniors, whether Jewish or non-Jewish, gay or straight, have much in common, more in common than they are different. The venerable senior lobbying organization the American Association of Retired Persons offers membership to those who are age fifty or over, without regard to religious affiliation or sexual orientation. Many businesses—hotels, theaters, and others offering "senior discounts"—characterize "seniors" as those over sixty-two. For decades after its inception, the Social Security system statutorily recognized sixty-five as the age of retirement. By statute, the age at which a senior now qualifies for Social Security benefits is, depending upon the year of birth, sixty-six years of age or older. Life expectancies having grown significantly, many "older people" remain in the workforce well into their eighties, and it is not uncommon to find some seniors continuing to work when they are ninety or over. Women still live longer than men. There is no single definition. In fact, there is a continuum on which older citizens find themselves at different stages of life. Many are caregivers for even more elderly parents. Many eighty-plus seniors are on the golf course, while others are homebound or in nursing homes.

Gays and lesbians are not much different from their heterosexual counterparts. They include young and active seniors as well as those who are old and frail. What is often significantly different is the relationships that they have with their families and with society in general. Gays, lesbians, bisexual, and transgender (GLBT) seniors today are very different from those GLBT baby boomers who will be elderly a generation from now. Many older gays today remember a closeted life, one filled with rightfully placed mistrust and danger, with lost families, lost jobs, lost housing, lost reputations, humiliation, and law enforcement threats. Hopefully, today, the younger GLBT generation has an expectation of openness, job opportunities, acceptance by family members, and legal and societal recognition of partners and children that did not exist when today's GLBT seniors were the same age. As a result, the needs of today's GLBT seniors are quite different from those that seniors in the future will face.

Many of today's GLBT seniors (perhaps most; there are no demographics to support conclusions based upon anecdotal experiences) do not have family members—children, siblings, or parents—to care for them as they age, to visit them in assisted-living facilities, to make the many decisions that must be made on behalf of dementia-affected elderly. For some, the close family members they do have may not be prepared to accept or acknowledge the sexual orientation or the gender identity of the GLBT senior. Moreover, the professional caregivers (e.g., medical practitioners, assisted-living or nursing home management and staff) may have only limited experience with any of the unique needs that the elderly GLBT person may have. In synagogues, senior citizen centers, and retirement and nursing homes, elderly GLBTs are often victimized in ways and for reasons not visited upon their heterosexual counterparts. Because of fear and caution, the elderly gay man or lesbian often feels isolated, unable to share life experiences—often the only joy an older person might have.

Society often refers to the "gay and lesbian community." The GLBT community is no more cohesive and monolithic than the "Jewish community," with people of different ages, education, family experiences growing up, socioeconomic backgrounds and current positions, religious affiliations (or nonaffiliations), political affiliations, and the like. While the majority of gays and lesbians do not have children and do not have partners, many older gays and lesbians were heterosexually married and have children, and younger gays and lesbians are choosing to have children. All of these differences influence their experiences as older adults.

As with their heterosexual counterparts, the difference between the single Jew and the part-nered Jew in the synagogue is enormous because their needs are so different. The synagogue, as never before, has become a place where age matters. Unfortunately, the synagogue is often a place that dispenses pediatric Judaism, focusing on young families, a place often hostile to the older congregant. If it is not hostile, then it is frequently dismissive. Many congregations do not see programming for older adults to be as important to the vitality of the synagogue as pro-gramming for children. In this respect, the older gay or lesbian Jew is not much different from any other older Jew. Yet within the synagogue as a *beit k'neset* for social interaction, the gay and lesbian Jew often feels as an outsider within a larger group of outsiders.

Most GLBTs stay away from synagogues for a variety of reasons, often for the same rea-sons as their heterosexual counterparts: long-held perceptions of hostility based upon bib-lical proscriptions, lifelong alienation from the larger Jewish community, fear, attitude ("What do I need that for? I have no children." "Why should I pay to belong to a place in which I am not welcome?" "I don't need the synagogue to identify myself as a Jew." "My income is limited. I can't afford to join"), and the like. Statistically, this is a reality, and while outreach to gay and lesbian Jews has often been quite successful, it has not been universally so. Many synagogues throughout the country are facing these same issues, without even see-ing the GLBT Jews among the seniors.

Younger active seniors, usually self-sufficient, find a multitude of interests and resources available and accessible. It is the single (gay or straight) and older seniors who have greater difficulties for which the synagogue could be a resource—intellectual, social, spiritual, reli-gious. The homebound or nursing home resident often has no access to the community experiences offered by the synagogue. The synagogue must provide services for senior Jews, regardless of orientation. Toward that goal, the synagogue must educate itself and its clergy, staff, layleaders, and congregants about GLBT Jews.

For those educational purposes, two important studies are recommended as resource material for congregations that would like to become open and welcoming to the older GLBT Jews in their communities. They are *Outing Age: Public Policy Issues Affecting Gay, Lesbian, Bisexual and Transgender Elders* and *Caregiving among Older Lesbian, Gay, Bisexual and Transgender New Yorkers*, the former compiled by the Policy Institute of the National Gay and Lesbian Task Force Foundation and the latter by the Policy Institute of the National Gay and Lesbian Task Force Foundation, Pride Senior Network, and Fordham University Graduate School of Social Service. Both are available online through the National Gay and Lesbian Task Force Foundation's Web site, **www.ngltf.org**.

Additional Resources

Books

Cohen, G. *The Creative Age: Awakening Human Potential in the Second Half of Life*. New York: Avon Books, 2000.

Cole, Thomas R. *The Journey of Life: A Cultural History of Aging in America*. Cambridge: Cambridge University Press, 1992.

Erikson, Erik H., Joan M. Erikson, and Helen Q. Kivnick. *Vital Involvement in Old Age*. New York: Norton, 1986.

Freed, Rachael. *Women's Lives, Women's Legacies: Passing Your Beliefs and Blessings to Future Generations, Creating Your Own Spiritual-Ethical Will*. Minneapolis: Fairview Press, 2003.

Friedman, Dayle A., ed. *Jewish Pastoral Care: A Practical Handbook from Traditional and Contemporary Sources*. Woodstock, VT: Jewish Lights Publishing, 2001.

Greenberg, Pearl. *Visual Arts and Older People: Developing Quality Programs*. Springfield, IL: C. Thomas, 1987.

Haight, B. K., and J. D. Webster, eds. *The Art and Science of Reminiscing: Theory, Research, Methods and Applications*. Washington, DC: Taylor & Francis, 1995.

Jacob, W. *Aging and the Aged in Jewish Law: Essays and Responsa*. New York: Rodef Shalom Press, 1998.

Jones, Jean Ellen. *Teaching Art to Older Adults: Guideline and Lessons*. Atlanta: Georgia State University, 1980.

Kimble, Melvin, ed. *Viktor Frankl's Contribution to Spirituality and Aging*. Binghamton, NY: Haworth Pastoral Press, 2001.

Kimble, Melvin A., and Susan H. McFadden, eds. *Aging, Spirituality and Religion: A Handbook*. Vols. 1 and 2. Minneapolis: Augsberg Fortress, 1995 and 2003.

Koenig, Harold G. *Aging and God: Spiritual Pathways to Mental Health in Midlife and Later Years*. Binghamton, NY: Haworth Press, 1994.

———. *Faith in the Future: Healthcare, Aging, and the Role of Religion*. West Conshohocken, PA: Templeton Press, 2004.

Lerman, Liz. *Teaching Dance to Senior Adults*. Springfield, IL: Thomas Press, 1984.

Lipschitz, David A. *Breaking the Rules of Aging*. Washington, DC: Lifeline Press, 2002.

Myerhoff, Barbara. *Number Our Days: A Triumph of Continuity and Culture Among Jewish Old People in an Urban Ghetto*. New York: Simon and Schuster, 1978.

Miller, Ronald S., and Zalman Schachter-Shalomi. *From Age-ing to Sage-ing: A Profound New Vision of Growing Older*. New York: Warner Books, 1995.

Moody, Harry R., and David Carroll, *The Five Stages of the Soul: Charting the Spiritual Passages that Shape Our Lives*. New York: First Anchor Books, 1998.

Roszak, Theodore. *Longevity Revolution: As Boomers Become Elders*. Berkeley, CA: Berkeley Hills Books, 2001.

Sales, Amy L. *Help, Opportunities and Programs for Jewish Elders: An Action Guide for Synagogues*. South Orange, NJ: The Grotta Foundation for Senior Care, 1998.

Silin, Peter S. *Nursing Homes: The Family's Journey*. Baltimore: Johns Hopkins University Press, 2001.

Waxman, Chaim I. *Jewish Baby Boomers: A Communal Perspective*. New York: SUNY Press, 2000.

Web Sites

Programming and Education

www.urj.org/educate/adults/: For the guide published by the URJ Department of Lifelong Jewish Learning, *Adult B'nei Mitzvah: Affirming Our Identity: A Guide for Facilitators* (New York: UAHC Press, 2001).

www.timeslips.org: For creative ideas on how to use storytelling as a way of assisting people who are suffering from dementia.

www.asaging.org: The American Society on Aging is dedicated to enhancing the knowledge and skills of laypersons working with older adults.

www.urj.org/njwhvc/renaissance: Renaissance Groups are geared to meet the social, cultural, and educational needs of older adults within our congregations. This program has been developed within the New Jersey/West Hudson Valley Council of the Union for Reform Judaism.

www.sageusa.org: SAGE is the oldest and largest social service and advocacy organization in the United States that works to support, empower, and celebrate gay, lesbian, bisexual, and transgender seniors.

www.ThirdAge.com: Third Age is a comprehensive Web site that provides a wide range of news, programming, and human interest issues for older adults.

www.NextAgeSpeakers.com: Next Age lists potential speakers for educational programs specific to issues of gerontology.

www.songwritingworks.org: Songwriting Works is an educational project of Judith Kate-Friedman of California. She has developed powerful programs that use elders' life experiences to fashion original songs. This is ideal for intergenerational as well as older adult programming.

www.huc.edu/kalsman: The Kalsman Institute on Judaism and Health, at the Hebrew Union College–Jewish Institute of Religion in Los Angeles, serves as an educational and training center for HUC-JIR students and alumni and for all people committed to spirituality and healing.

www.hiddur.org: HIDDUR: Center for Aging and Judaism of Reconstructionist Rabbinical College in Wyncote, Pennsylvania, provides professional training, program development, consultation, and direct service to foster lives of meaning, connection, and celebration for Jewish elders and their caregivers.

www.sacredseasons.org: Hiddur also has developed Jewish spiritual resources for older adults in their "Sacred Seasons" program, designed to introduce Jewish traditions and rituals to people in residential facilities.

Housing Options

www.myziva.net: For caregivers and seniors who want to easily find, evaluate, and compare nursing homes in their local community.

www.aahsa.org: The American Association of Homes and Services for the Aging is committed to advancing the vision of healthy, affordable, and ethical aging services.

www.ajas.org: The Association of Jewish Aging Services of North America is an excellent resource to begin evaluating the option of creating an independent senior housing development.

Conclusion

The goal of our project on Sacred Aging is really quite simple. It is to raise awareness within congregations to the reality that the world of the older adult has changed. This new multi-generational cohort represents the majority of our membership, a vast untapped reservoir of life experience with a seemingly insatiable desire for meaningful Jewish experiences. What also seems likely is that if the synagogue does not provide these responses, they will go and create it on their own. In many ways, *To Honor and Respect* is a guidebook for developing a membership retention program for congregations.

At the beginning of the twenty-first century, the North American Jewish community finds itself in the midst of a great age of transition. This reflects the overwhelming social, political, economic, and religious transitions that are taking place outside of the Jewish community. Change, it seems, is the only constant. Yet what remains the same is the desire for our life to mean something, to stand for something, and for us to acquire a sense of purpose. The synagogue remains the central address for these goals to be met, for our dreams to be fulfilled. The current revolution in gerontology, as with any revolution, requires us to rethink and revision. It means that we must not fear to take risks, to remember the faith in the future that Abraham showed and that Nachshon lived. The emerging generations of older adults want and need their synagogues to be places where their dreams are welcomed and their lives are validated. They deserve our synagogues to be open, welcoming, and affirming of their lives, no matter what age they may be or what stage of life they find themselves. To be any less, to forget our legacies will reduce the contemporary synagogue to irrelevancy, a mere service institution that processes people through various life-cycle events without a sense of transcendent meaning or historical linkage.

The revolution that is before us calls all of us to one additional arena of concern. In the United States there exist debates over various issues related to the economics of aging. Countless hours of discussion and articles and books now flood us on issues of Social Security and Medicare reform. They miss the real issue. We need to arm our congregational social justice committees to call for a total revision of how our society looks at what it means to age. To divide the discussion will weaken the process. We, as the richest society in the world, need to take a "holistic" approach to issues such as health, access to medical care, funding, end-of-life decisions, nutrition, caregiving, and the way society looks at, honors, and respects the aging.

Finally, a word of hope. The revolution in longevity is exciting and presents us with unbelievable opportunities for creativity, caring, education, and communal transformation. We hope that congregations will take some of the ideas of this book and shape them according to their own congregational culture. What we urge you to do, however, is to *do it!*